D1321073

A guide to the London Countryway

Also by Keith Chesterton
with W. G. Byrnes

Decisions, strategies and new ventures (1973)

A guide to
the London Countryway

Keith Chesterton

Constable London

First published in Great Britain 1978
by Constable and Company Ltd
10 Orange Street London WC2H 7EG
Copyright © 1978 Keith Chesterton

Second edition 1981

ISBN 0 09 461740 6

Set in Monophoto Times New Roman 9pt
Filmset and printed in Great Britain by
BAS Printers Limited, Over Wallop, Hampshire

Preface to second edition

Regrettably, despite the damage they are doing to the countryside, motorways are still being extended and one important change has been made in the Countryway route to avoid them. It now goes via Theydon Bois rather than Epping, with a 3-mile section rerouted. A new map has also been provided for a difficult stretch by Stapleford Tawney.

Transport and opening-times have been checked and the accommodation list has been thoroughly revised, with all prices checked and a number of new addresses inserted, especially in Surrey. Many of these changes have been suggested to me by readers of this book and I would like to thank them for the trouble they have taken. Happy Walking.

K. Chesterton

Contents

Maps

The twenty-two Bartholomew's 1:100 000 maps appear at the beginning of each of the relevant sections of the London Countryway. These maps are reproduced with the permission of Messrs. Bartholomew.

Key for maps

– – – –	footpath
= = = =	farm-track/bridleway
▅▅▅▅	road
∿∿∿	stream
——	field boundary/hedge/fence
┼┼┼	railway line
⅄⅄⅄	wooded area
FB	footbridge
∎	house/public house/farm etc.
S	stile
FPS	footpath sign
G	gate
P.H	public house
T	toilets
N.T.	National Trust

Countryway route marked ▬ ▬ ▬ ▬ ▬

(footpath, farm-track/bridleway, road grouped as Countryway route marked)

The Long Distance Walkers Association backed the idea of the London Countryway when I first suggested it to them and its members surveyed the way, produced route descriptions and checked them. Without their aid, production of this route would have taken many years more.

Fred Tarrant checked half the initial route description and Tom and Anne Anderson and Pearl and George Bull walked the Countryway after the first description had been published and sent me details of corrections. I would thank especially Jeff Ellingham who organized the work while I was in the USA for a period, walked the whole way and produced many valuable changes to the initial route.

Brian Graves has drawn the maps in this book, specially surveying the different areas to do so, and without his skill the book would be much poorer. Julie Royce and my wife, Jill, typed the book between them and I am very grateful for their hard work.

Lastly I would like to thank the large number of people who are not named but who have helped considerably— footpath secretaries for guidance on certain rights of way, many people on the route for information and a welcome, and my friends for bearing my talk of this walk for so long without complaint. I hope that the finished work is some reward to them all.

OUTLINE MAP OF THE LONDON COUNTRYWAY

The London Countryway is a new, continuous, footpath
route in the countryside round London, completely encircling
it. It has been designed to be near enough to London to have
good transport to all parts of the route yet far enough out to
avoid suburbia and to pass through some of the best country
round London. The nearest point on the route to the centre of
London is by Waltham Abbey, when it is 13 miles from
Charing Cross, and its furthest is 31 miles away at West
Wycombe, behind High Wycombe. The Countryway can be
walked in one continuous expedition—and has been—but its
length of 205 miles and its location is likely to make this a
minority interest.

Most people will want to do the walk in a series of day-
outings, with perhaps, the occasional week-end away. The
route is ideal for this with forty or so railway stations and
six youth hostels within a mile of the way. It could be
treated as a challenge, but there are so many fascinating
places to look round and such good views that it seems rather
a waste to try and rush it too much.

Outline of route
The Countryway is a circular walk so it can be started
anywhere, but Box Hill gives a good start and an even better
finish. From Box Hill the route goes from the Stepping Stones
through a variety of different woods over Ranmore Common
and Hackhurst downs to the beech glades of Sheepleas. There
is then a flatter stretch by several commons and parts of the
Wey and Basingstoke canals to leave Surrey by Windsor Park
and reach Windsor. After looking round Windsor castle, the
walker has 7 miles by the Thames to Maidenhead and then by
the lovely old village of Cookham to Marlow. The Chilterns
start here and the route goes up and down the hills and
through the beech woods for 30 miles. It passes the National
Trust village of West Wycombe and goes by Great Missenden
and Chipperfield Common with its Apostles Pool, to cross the
Grand Union canal at Kings Langley.

The next place is St Albans, where there is so much to see
with the Roman wall and theatre, the Cathedral, museum, old
streets and pubs that a rest day is almost called for—though I
find sightseeing much more exhausting than footpath walking.
The route from St Albans gives a peaceful section through the
Hertfordshire countryside, passing some pleasant villages and
pubs, North Mymms Park and the Swallowhole where the
Mimmshall brook vanishes into the ground. Next comes
Wormley wood, with its difficult navigation, before
Broxbourne and the Lea Valley Regional Park. The Lea
Valley is something you either love or hate but Waltham
Abbey at its end appeals to everyone with its marvellous
decoration. Epping Forest follows, still beautiful despite the
efforts of the road makers, and then a series of isolated old
churches across the Essex countryside to Brentwood. There
are two country parks to go through by Brentwood and then
a long section through the flat Essex fens, quite different from
anywhere else. It is lonely and hard going but has hidden
away Orsett and West Tilbury, two unknown but fascinating
places.

The route crosses the Thames by the Tilbury–Gravesend
ferry and goes along the chalk and sandstone hills of Kent to
the Surrey border. It gives magnificent views over the Weald
and passes near Cobham with its Dickens associations, the
neolithic Coldrum Stones, Tudor Ightham Mote and Knole
Park. The final stretch through Surrey again is along the line
of the North Downs and gives splendid walking on the short
turf, and by old ways through the yews and junipers at the
bottom of the hills.

Places on the way
The Countryway is much more than a country walk; there are
so many old houses, churches, pubs and curiosities on the
route. I thought I knew the area round London fairly well,
but walking this route and discovering the places on it and the
events that happened in them gave me a new feeling
altogether. The people associated with the route make a
fascinating mixture. There are the Royals of course, with

Charles II, George IV and Queen Victoria especially
associated with Windsor Castle. Elizabeth I was being held at
Hatfield when she was told she had become Queen, and she
made her famous speech before the Spanish Armada at
Tilbury. King Harold founded Waltham Abbey, King
Edmund's body rested at Greensted, Queen Boadicea
attacked St Albans and King Offa founded the abbey there.
Bishop Cedd made the first Christian mission from Tilbury
and Britain's only Pope, Adrian IV, was born at Bedmond,
near St Albans.

Then there are the famous. Lord Nelson said goodbye to
Lady Hamilton at Box Hill and Sir Walter Raleigh's head is
buried at Horsley. Francis Dashwood, the radical M.P., had
the house, mausoleum and church built at West Wycombe,
Disraeli lived at Bradenham and Hughenden Manor and
General Wolfe's house and statue are at Westerham. And the
route passes right by the best known, perhaps, of all, Winston
Churchill's home at Chartwell.

The most welcome discoveries are about some of those
who struggled for the liberties that we now enjoy. William
Grindcobbe and the hedge priest, John Ball, were both hanged
at St Albans after the Peasants' Revolt, and Jack Cade
defeated the King's army in Knole Park in the 1450 rebellion.
John Hampden of Hampden, near Prestwood, was one of the
five M.P.s Charles I tried to arrest in Parliament, and Sir John
Vane of Fairlawne was executed by Charles II for insisting on
the rights of Parliament. Much later, the Tolpuddle Martyrs
were resettled in Greensted after being brought back from
their transportation to Australia. Two valiant fighters of
particular interest for readers of this book were Octavia Hill,
one of the founders of the National Trust, who is buried at
Crockham Hill, and Thomas Willingale of Loughton who
suffered in jail for fighting for the rights of the commoners in
Epping Forest. Perhaps John Tyme, leading the struggle
against motorways, will be able to join this distinguished list.

Lastly, there are the literary and artistic connections:
Dickens and *The Pickwick Papers* at Cobham, Bulldog
Drummond at Maidenhead, Meredith who lived at the foot of
Box Hill, Little Miss Muffet at North Mymms, Delius's grave

at Limpsfield and Stanley Spencer and his paintings at
Cookham. There are many more, too—all the host of people
who have lived and worked in this area near London,
influenced strongly by the city but not a part of it. Some of
those are mentioned in the book but most live on only in the
buildings and country left behind and in the part they
played—big or small—in making it like it is today.

Like the people, the buildings and dwellings have a variety
that would be difficult to find anywhere else. They are of all
ages, from neolithic man to the present day, and range from
the magnificent buildings of kings, bishops and great
landowners to the houses, churches, roads and inns in
everyday use. There is Windsor Castle and the glorious St
George's chapel, the great nave of St Albans cathedral and
Waltham Abbey with its pre-Raphaelite decoration. For great
houses, there are Knole House, the largest private house in
England, in its splendid park, West Wycombe house with its
associated church and caves, and Ightham Mote, that superb
Tudor building and moat. And there is also, again, Chartwell,
not large in the same way as these, but full of the atmosphere
of Churchill. From pre-Norman times, there are the Roman
wall, theatre and hypocaust at St Albans, Ambersbury Banks
in Epping Forest, a neolithic burial chamber at Coldrum
Stones in Kent and the beautiful Saxon timber church at
Greensted.

The area is extraordinarily rich in churches. As well as
those mentioned already, there are, for instance, Cobham
church and its brasses in Kent, the lonely churches of Essex,
St Mary's at West Horsley and Cookham church with Stanley
Spencer's painting of the Last Supper. With inns and pubs we
have even more to choose from: there are the ancient inns of
West Wycombe, Oxted and St Albans, particularly the Fleur-
de-Lys and the Goat, there is that Edwardian survival, the
Feathers at Merstham, the Barley Mow and its shove-
ha'penny at Horsley, the busy and boisterous King's Arms in
Epping and Ferry Inn at Cookham, the Amazon and Tiger in
Harvel, a quiet village pub with good real ale, and many
others that offer nothing special except for a resting place, a
drink, some food and a welcome.

There are the gardens—the Royal Horticultural Society at Wisley, the Rose Society near St Albans and Emmetts in Kent. Then there are all those interesting places that rather defy classification, such as the Totem Pole and the Leptis Magna ruins in Windsor Park, Tilbury fort on the Thames and the tiny Gatton town hall in Surrey. This last is the place A. J. P. Taylor selected as the one that would tell a foreign visitor most about England.

I could carry on this litany of places, but fear it would take away your pleasure in discovering them as you walk. I hope I've written just enough to entice you.

How it all began
Considering, indeed, how many places there are to see, it's rather surprising how slowly it all started. In 1971 I lived on the Kent edge of London and was a member of a local walking club. This had a mixture of different length rambles in our local countryside of Kent and eastern Surrey, enlivened by a few week-ends away. Some of those had been used by the group to do long walks like the North Downs and South Downs Ways a week-end at a time, and I was musing over some maps and wondering what new walk we could do like this. The club had invented one or two of its own and I was trying to find another, reasonably nearby, when I thought, why not make a continuous walk round London? There was good countryside—the Surrey and Kent hills and the Chilterns—and it would be easy to travel there and back.

I put the idea to the next committee meeting, but to my surprise, the others did not share my enthusiasm. They wanted to get away from London for their week-end trips and felt that this walk would be just like the normal day's outing. I retired hurt, but still thought it was a good idea and worked out a few possibilities on maps. Then the ramblers' magazine, *Rucksack*, appeared with an article on European long-distance paths which included mention of a circular route round Paris. I thought if there is a footpath round Paris, there can certainly be a better one round London, with its superior and more varied countryside.

I sent a letter to *Rucksack*, giving the idea, outlining the route and asking for helpers. I had ten replies, so I knew there must be others who liked the idea. Unfortunately I then moved to Surrey and I did little until I came into contact with members of a new organization, the Long Distance Walkers Association, which I had joined. The founder members lived in Surrey, and I put my idea to them and they agreed to back it. I had found fellow enthusiasts and started work—though if I had realized quite how much work I was letting myself in for, and how long it would take, I wouldn't have been quite so eager!

The original idea was to use the existing North Downs Way and the Ridgeway and to find new routes only to link them, but after a few trials we abandoned this. The Ridgeway seemed too far out, and anyway it seemed better to use different paths and not get the same ones too well used. I worked out different routes on the map and had volunteers trying them out on the ground and producing a first description. We then walked them out and decided whether to keep the route or alter it. Some sections we had a great deal of trouble with—we had five different goes to get round Woking till we found the solution of using the canals. One person particularly, Jeff Ellingham, did a very large amount of work trying out alternatives, especially when I left the country for a period.

The whole idea was to take the route through as attractive countryside as possible and to avoid roads as much as we could. We were using existing rights of way, and places with public access, so this involved some tortuous route-taking on occasion, but we managed to finish with less than 20 miles of road in total. (There were just two sections with an appreciable stretch of road, through Brentwood and Gravesend.) Finally, after checking and rechecking the routes and the description, we were able to bring out the completed route in early 1976, five years after the first idea. The walk was designed with scenery in mind, with ease of transport as a secondary factor. Historic places and stately homes were not considered initially, except for Chartwell, West Wycombe and St Albans, but when we considered alternatives, I did take this into account.

Other routes round London

The idea of a walk round London is a simple and attractive one and has occurred to other people besides myself. But I have met no one who had done it nor have I seen such an attempt in print. The nearest plan is in a book kindly given to me by L. M. Nicholson of Guildford. This is called *Country Walks in Greater London, being the circuit of the Metropolis by lane, footpath, field and ferry,* and was written by a Dr Greenfields and published in 1909. Dr Greenfields's route was much closer in than mine, and lay between 8 and 12 miles from Charing Cross. The nearest point of his route to mine lies in the Lea Valley where he goes by Enfield Lock, 1 mile from Waltham Abbey. He was rather keener on roads than I am—presumably they were much more pleasant then—and, for some curious reason, his route does not completely encircle London. He left a gap between Barking and Lee in south London, so this book can still claim to be an account of the first complete walk!

However, I hope it won't be the last. I think my route is a good one, but after walking it, try one of your own. There are a host of different footpaths in the London area and an almost incalculable number of ways of joining them up to make a complete circuit. Some of these paths I have tried and not used because of difficulties of obstructions or of description, but don't let that inhibit you. Happy walking!

Doing the walk

The Countryway is designed for walking in a series of days out, or at week-ends with a night away from home, or the whole way can be walked in a holiday. There are advantages to each method and the book has been written for all types of walker. The easiest and simplest way for those living in the London area is to do it by days and the walk has been split into twenty-two stages for this. Each one is between 7 and 13 miles long and makes a good day's walk for the slower walker or one who wants to do a lot of sightseeing on the way. The faster walker may well wish to do two stages at a time and would probably choose to finish sometimes at places other than those suggested. There is ample scope to vary stopping-off points with so many stations and radial bus routes on the way. To do the walk thus provides a challenge over a good period of time: a quite different experience is had when walking the whole route at once.

When one is taking a holiday and walking the way, it is surprising how one seems in a totally different world from that of the commuter and work. Despite being so near London, I felt like a tourist in a foreign country seeing familiar routines being done in an unfamiliar way. I was watching the men rush to the station to catch their train to work, the women take children to school and the milkman chat to his customers, all carrying on their own lives quite separate from me, the passing stranger. I gained a greater sense of peace and relaxation from them and from seeing the local sights than from many a conventional holiday farther away. It has much to recommend it and the only drawback is finding accommodation.

Accommodation is listed at the end of each stage, but some places offer very little. In these areas the walker has to be flexible on what type of accommodation he or she wants. There are six youth hostels on the route with three others accessible, so hostellers can walk the route fairly easily. There are one or two gaps, though, particularly round Tilbury and Gravesend where they will need to use alternatives or travel rather a long way to a hostel. There are also a few official camp sites on the route, though gaps occur in the same places as with hostels; however, there are many places on the way where a careful and considerate camper can put up a tent for a night without disturbing anyone. The chief difficulty is in obtaining water and a good-sized water container is desirable.

At the other end of the scale, there are a number of more expensive hotels in the larger towns and motels on the main roads, particularly on the western side of the route. It is the cheaper hotels, guest houses and bed-and-breakfast places that are difficult to find. However, some do exist, particularly near Maidenhead, St Albans, Windsor and Maidstone and details of these and of other types of accommodation are given in an appendix. Despite this, careful planning is needed, especially on the eastern side of the Countryway, so as to finish each day at a place with convenient accommodation or with an easy journey to it.

Preferences for distances and comfort will determine what is a good schedule for each walker, and I have tried to give sufficient detail to make this choice an informed one. Although I am offering one way of doing the walk, there are many other possibilities.

A holiday fortnight

Day 1	Merstham to Tanners Hatch Y.H.	12 miles
Day 2	Tanners Hatch to West Byfleet. Stay there or at Woking or Guildford	14½ miles
Day 3	West Byfleet to Windsor	18 miles
Day 4	Windsor to West Wycombe. Stay there or at Bradenham Y.H.	21 miles
Day 5	West Wycombe to Lee Gate Y.H.	10 miles
Day 6	Lee Gate to St Albans	20½ miles
Day 7	Rest day at St Albans	
Day 8	St Albans to Newgate Street. Stay at Hertford (or on to Broxbourne for extra 7 miles and stay at Harlow Y.H.)	15 miles
Day 9	Newgate Street to Epping Forest Y.H.	14 miles
Day 10	Epping to Brentwood	17½ miles
Day 11	Brentwood to Gravesend	18½ miles
Day 12	Gravesend to Borough Green. Stay at Kemsing Y.H. or in the West Malling area.	16 miles
Day 13	Borough Green to Crockham Hill Y.H.	14½ miles
Day 14	Crockham Hill Y.H. to Merstham	13½ miles

The book starts the walk from Box Hill, but starting from Merstham allows the first night to be spent at Tanners Hatch Hostel, or Dorking. The distances are approximate as they depend on the exact place where the night is spent.

Week-end walks

Doing the walk by week-ends provides a good compromise. It gives the pleasure of being away for a night and cuts down on travelling expenses, yet avoids many of the accommodation problems. The route can be split so as to provide a good place to stay on the Saturday and to travel back on the Sunday from the difficult places. There are more options still and the occasional day out can be interspersed in the week-ends—particularly if you live near the route.

A good walk can be made using the fortnight's holiday schedule as a basis.

1st week-end   Days 1 and 2—avoiding difficulties at West Byfleet.

2nd week-end   Finish Sunday at Marlow.

3rd week-end   Saturday Marlow to West Wycombe and Sunday to Great Missenden or Ashley Green.

4th week-end   Saturday walk to St Albans and on Sunday to Newgate Street.

5th week-end   Days 9 and 10, travelling back on Sunday from Brentwood.

6th week-end   Days 11 and 12. There may still be a little travelling to find accommodation on the Saturday.

7th week-end   Days 13 and 14.

The journey between West Wycombe and St Albans can be split between the two week-ends, depending on how much time is wanted to look round St Albans.

Walking the way

The London Countryway is a footpath route using existing rights of way and public access land, and is not a specially designated or 'official' route. There are no special signposts pointing the way, just the standard footpath or bridleway signs provided, (or not, as the case may be) by the appropriate Council. I have tried to avoid obstructed paths, but this has not always proved possible, particularly in Essex. The route is as easy or hard to follow as others in the same district, though with time one would expect it to become clearer than the average. The vast majority of the paths used are clear and easy to follow, but there is some barbed wire and certain of them do seem to get ploughed and planted over. This seems to happen regularly on stages 14 and 16. Whenever this occurs, try to follow the instructions—making sure you *are* on the right route—note the location and type of obstruction and report it to the local council. It would help if you could also tell the Ramblers' Association who would follow up your complaint for you. It does make the way less like following a clear trail and more of a walk you are enjoying on your own.

Considerable trouble has been taken in producing this book to provide a clear and accurate written description of the entire route, and it should be possible to follow the way with this alone. In addition, the whole route is given on 1:100 000 scale maps (1 inch to 1.6 miles) with the more complicated portions on 1:25 000 scale ($2\frac{1}{2}$ inches to 1 mile). These should enable the walk to be followed with no other assistance or equipment, but it is useful to have a compass and know how to use it—especially in woods.

Navigation

To use a compass with the accuracy required of this walk, or most other walks, is very simple if a modern Silva-type compass is used.

All directions given in the text are magnetic bearings (1977), so no corrections are required.

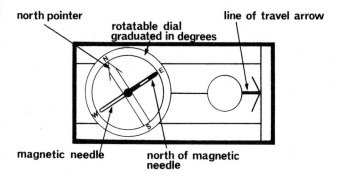

north pointer

rotatable dial graduated in degrees

line of travel arrow

magnetic needle

north of magnetic needle

A TYPICAL COMPASS

To follow a given bearing:
1. Rotate the dial till the line-of-travel arrow points on the bearing indicated—130° in the example.

2. Turn the whole compass so that the North of the magnetic needle lies over the North pointer.

3. Hold the compass and note the direction the line-of-travel arrow is pointing in. Pick out something in that direction—a tall tree, a house or a hedge.

4. Head towards the object picked out, occasionally checking by the compass.

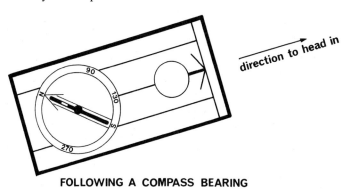

direction to head in

FOLLOWING A COMPASS BEARING

Grid references

To help the walker get back to the route, if the way is lost, a
large number of place names and grid references have been
put in the route description. These can be used to find the
nearest point on the route to where the walker is and a way
back to it. Instructions on how to understand a grid reference
are on every O.S. map.

Clothing

The route goes over ordinary field paths and hills in the south
of England so no special clothing of any kind is necessary, nor
large clumpy boots. Fields can get muddy, even in summer, so
it is useful to have shoes with some ankle protection or light
boots, but many experienced walkers prefer light training
shoes and simply dodge the wet patches. In wetter weather,
two plastic bags to put over each foot, or a spare pair of
shoes, are desirable to keep mud from pub or café carpets. If
you are going to walk in the rain, a waterproof over-garment
such as a cagoule or plastic mac, and waterproof over-
trousers are useful to have. A small rucksack to put these and
your sandwiches in complete the necessary gear. If you are
going to stay overnight, make the rucksack slightly larger and
carry your spare clothes in it.

How to use this book

This book is arranged to be of maximum use for all methods
of walking the Countryway. All the information on each stage
of the walk is together, and the account of features of interest
and people associated with the area is kept separate from the
detailed route description—this avoids confusion when the
walk is being followed. The information necessary for
planning the walk is collected together at the end of each
stage. It lists train frequencies for stations on the route and
bus services where there are no trains. It also gives buses
which link back to earlier stages of the route—particularly
useful if a car is used to get to a start point. Times of opening
are given for National Trust houses and other places open to
the public, so that a stage can be planned for the right time

and day to see them. Refreshment places are listed, and the location given if it is not obvious. Places where accommodation can be found are given, but addresses are put in an appendix, as one place can be used for more than one stage and addresses are rather lengthy.

There are 1:25 000 maps for difficult areas. These have been specially surveyed and drawn for this book and should be more accurate for the route than O.S. maps. The 1:100 000 maps for the rest of the route, together with the route description, should be perfectly adequate for following the way. However, if you want to try a diversion, or stray off the route, or want to know what is in a distant view, it is advisable to obtain the relevant O.S. 1:50 000 maps. Those required are given for each stage, but if you wish to collect them all, you will need numbers 165, 166, 167, 175, 177, 186, 187 and 188. Numbers 167 and 186 only cover very small portions of the route. If you still have or can obtain 1-inch maps, five will suffice, numbers 159, 160, 161, 170 and 171.

Errors and alterations

Great care has been taken to get the route description, maps and information as accurate as possible. The route description, in particular, has been used in the field over a period of nine months and comments received from this incorporated in the text. Nevertheless, there may still be some errors in it and alterations are occurring all the time in the countryside. After the first route description was published, one roundabout was removed, a bypass built and a housing estate built over a footpath, as well as lesser alterations elsewhere. Although the paths used in this book are public (except in the few cases where it is noted as permissive use only), diversion orders can be made. These are very rare though, and much less common than the cases where the owner says a diversion has been made when it hasn't. I would be grateful for notice of any errors or alterations found (via the publisher) but please make sure you are in the right place first! Details of opening hours also change, so if you want to be absolutely certain do check.

Unfortunately, prices change frequently and are liable to be incorrect when this book is published. Those given here were valid in 1977 and can be taken as a comparative guide to present-day costs.

Recommendations
The details of any accommodation are given as received by me and although I have tried out little of it myself, I have no reason to believe it is not suitable. I have tried out many more of the refreshment places mentioned, but not all, and the proprietor or his attitudes may have changed since my visit, either for better or worse. Fortunately, walking is on the upsurge after a bad patch in the 1960s and proprietors are now more anxious to please walkers and other non-motorists!

Style
The route descriptions use metres throughout, for all distances under a mile. For most purposes yards can be used as a substitute, but metres are more convenient for map and compass. With admittedly, a certain lack of consistency, I have used miles for longer distances—miles seem to mean more in giving the length of a walk!

Bearings given in the text are *magnetic* bearings. These do not need a correction and will be sufficiently accurate for eighty years!

Distances

Stage	Start	Finish	Distance (in miles)	Total (in miles)	Distance to station at end	Page
1	Box Hill	Horsley	9	9	—	33
2	Horsley	West Byfleet	$8\frac{1}{2}$	$17\frac{1}{2}$	—	43
3	West Byfleet	Sunningdale	9	$26\frac{1}{2}$	$\frac{1}{2}$	51
4	Sunningdale	Windsor	9	$35\frac{1}{2}$	—	59
5	Windsor	Marlow	13	$48\frac{1}{2}$	$\frac{1}{2}$	69
6	Marlow	West Wycombe	8	$56\frac{1}{2}$	$2\frac{1}{2}$	81
7	West Wycombe	Gt Missenden	8	$64\frac{1}{2}$	$\frac{1}{2}$	91
8	Gt Missenden	Ashley Green	7	$71\frac{1}{2}$	2	101
9	Ashley Green	Kings Langley	$8\frac{1}{2}$	80	—	111
10	Kings Langley	St Albans	7	87	$\frac{3}{4}$	121
11	St Albans	Brookmans Park	$10\frac{1}{2}$	$97\frac{1}{2}$	$\frac{1}{2}$	133
12	Brookmans Park	Broxbourne	$11\frac{1}{2}$	109	—	145
13	Broxbourne	Theydon Bois	11	120	—	155
14	Theydon Bois	Bentley	$9\frac{1}{2}$	$129\frac{1}{2}$	3	167
15	Bentley	West Horndon	9	$138\frac{1}{2}$	—	177
16	West Horndon	East Tilbury	$8\frac{1}{2}$	147	$\frac{1}{2}$	185
17	East Tilbury	Sole Street	11	158	—	193
18	Sole Street	Borough Green	10	168	$\frac{3}{4}$	205
19	Borough Green	Ide Hill	$10\frac{1}{2}$	$178\frac{1}{2}$	4	217
20	Ide Hill	Hurst Green	$8\frac{1}{2}$	187	$\frac{1}{2}$	233
21	Hurst Green	Merstham	9	196	—	245
22	Merstham	Box Hill	9	205	$\frac{1}{2}$	255

This opening stage of the walk gives an exhilarating start with good climbs up to Ranmore Common, views across the Surrey hills and some interesting old places to visit. The start of the walk is near Box Hill station at the Stepping Stones over the River Mole. The stepping stones are a favourite spot on week-end afternoons in a hot summer. Children delight in crossing them and they make a good photograph. There is a bridge slightly downstream for the rare occasions when the Mole is in flood. In spite of its popularity it is still a pleasant place, and you are well served for refreshments. If you feel like starting at the top of Box Hill rather than at the bottom, there are the very pleasant Fort Tea Rooms where you can enjoy your snack in the open air. Just a little along the road is a car park with another refreshment stall and, for a fuller meal, the Burford Bridge Hotel where Nelson said goodbye to Emma, Lady Hamilton, before Trafalgar. If you are going on this walk alone you could well say goodbye to your own mistress (or other loved ones) here. With luck you may do better than Nelson and come back alive—you will be more likely to do so if you look carefully before you cross the busy A24.

You then go by footpaths through the Denbies estate, open every day except 31 December, and very pleasant too. The North Downs Way is intended to go through here, but at the time of writing, there is still argument about the exact route. Towards the top there is a prolific bracken crop which, when not harvested, provides an excellent playground for dogs. At the top you pass Ranmore Church, designed by Sir Gilbert Scott, but only occasionally open to visitors. On the right there is a path to Tanners Hatch Youth Hostel, through Ranmore Common, a large expanse of beech woods. The hostel, converted from two old cottages, is a pleasant informal one, with oil lamps, wood fire and an enthusiastic Warden who has produced his own orienteering course in the woods. A delightful place to stay, unless you are fussy about everything being in perfect order. There is a view from near the hostel of Polesden Lacey, a fine Palladian villa, built in

1823. If you are making this day's walk a short one you should certainly go and have a look at the house, its pottery collection and its fine gardens, although it may be very crowded on summer Sundays. Sheridan used to own this house, now in the care of the National Trust.

Back on the route, you go across a field owned again by the National Trust, where you will get a fine view if you go 100 metres to the top of the slope. Dorking is spread out on the left, a pleasant little town, and behind, a long range of sandstone hills—Leith Hill, Holmbury Hill, Pitch Hill and over in the distance on the right, Black Down, easily picked out by its characteristic steep drop. Next there is a long narrow path between trees, which some people find oppressive and others attractive. It is the future line of the North Downs Way and there are good views on the left through occasional gaps in the trees.

There are also little posts marking a nature trail. There are, apparently, leaflets describing this on the Ranmore Common Road but I have never been lucky enough to find one. The yellow paint marks are probably the remains of an old Tanners Hatch marathon route. This is the most popular walking marathon in the country and it takes place on the first Sunday of every July, when around a thousand people take part. Starting from Tanners Hatch Youth Hostel or Leatherhead football ground, the aim is to cover 30 miles of Surrey country in ten hours, with a different route each year. A 50-mile-long walk (to be done in fifteen hours) is also organized every other year.

After the straight section, the path bends round a combe and we come to the first of the many pill boxes we will meet. There is a whole line of these near the bottom slope of the downs, put there at the beginning of the Second World War to act as a line of defence if the German army were to break through from the Channel. They are still very substantial and more adventurous children play in them. The path wanders on the boundary between trees and scrub. It can be hard to follow the exact route, but it is a fascinating path. There are a number of deer in the woods, but these are mostly seen in the

White Downs in the Snow

early morning or at dusk. Later we go by Hackhurst Downs, owned by the Surrey County Council as an 'open space' but it is mostly covered by scrub. Surrey is fortunate in having many open spaces and this is one of its most attractive. Buried deep in the woods are some of the largest primroses I have seen: if you find them, leave them to prosper. You can be very alone up here if you wish. I have picnicked here in the height of summer in a secluded spot and peacefully watched the world going past in the valley below.

To the north of this, you come to a junction of six paths at Blind Oak Gate. There used to be views, but the growth of the trees and new forestry has removed them. It can still seem a remote spot well away from the common image of Surrey as entirely covered by houses. There are one or two old metalled roads about, built during the war for the Canadians who were stationed here; it is interesting to see how firm they are after thirty years without maintenance. After Honeysuckle Bottom, where I have not seen any honeysuckle, one goes up a steep path to the appropriately named Mountain Wood. Past here we come to Sheepleas, another Surrey open space, particularly attractive in autumn with its many woodland glades and superb beech trees. Sheepleas is popular locally but not much known elsewhere: there was a proposal to build a public lavatory here for visitors but this was fiercely opposed by the locals on the grounds that it would spoil the countryside and attract undesirables. I hope you will not be regarded as an undesirable here—it is something to ponder about on the walk why people who, as individuals, are concerned for others forget this when they act collectively. At the end of Sheepleas is St Mary's Church, West Horsley. This is a charming old church, with twelfth-century tower, thirteenth-century chancel and several interesting wall paintings.

After Sir Walter Raleigh was executed, his widow, who lived in this area, obtained his head, boiled it and carried it round with her for the rest of her life in a small leather bag. It is supposed to be buried in the churchyard, but the only local memory of his name is in the nearby Raleigh School.

On the right along the A246, is the thirteenth-century St Martin's Church, East Horsley, which ought to be famous as

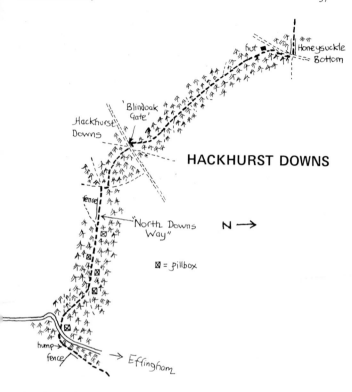

the place where Lady Lovelace daughter of Lord Byron and
collaborator with Charles Babbage, the nineteenth-century
computer pioneer, is buried. Next door to it is Horsley
Towers, a Gothic building built in the nineteenth-century and
now used by the Electricity Council for training, but
occasionally seen in TV plays substituting for a Teutonic
castle. Continuing the walk, you come to West Horsley where
there are two pleasant pubs. The nearest is the Barley Mow
which has a large public bar with stone flagged floor,
dartboard and shove-ha'penny table—bring your own
ha'pennies. The section finishes after a walk by the railway
line to East Horsley station, where there are frequent services

to London or Guildford. There are several shops here and a steak bar at the Horsley Hotel.

Route

The start is at the stepping stones over the River Mole at the foot of Boxhill (173513). The best access is from Boxhill station, 800 metres away. Right out of station and in 300 metres reach A24. Under road by tunnel, turn right along it, in 500 metres by the side of playing fields go left on a rough track through trees to reach stepping stones in 200 metres. These are occasionally under water but there is a footbridge 100 metres to the left.

Now for the route proper. Retrace steps to A24. Bear left across A24 to metalled track behind bus stop into Denbies estate (closed 31 December). Under railway (168513), and past lodge. (For Boxhill station: after 400 metres, opposite stile on left, take path on right and then right on the road.) Keep on up to T-junction where go left. Ignore left fork 30 metres on but go right at cross tracks 100 metres later, and on up to clearing, where fork right past telegraph pole following orange way marks. Cross road, continue on and bear right along next road (wide verge). Soon pass Ranmore Church. 100 metres on, at road junction, cross to stile behind National Trust sign. (For Tanners Hatch Youth Hostel, continue on for 300 metres and past cottage on right. Right and follow waymarks for 1,200 metres to hostel.) Over second stile into field. Go right, keeping hedge on right, and cross stile into woods. Keep ahead on a long straight track for 1,000 metres ignoring cross tracks and following yellow paint, until track swings right uphill. Here follow yellow paint route straight ahead. When track comes in from right, bear left downhill. At pillbox bear right up path and keep to same height for 600 metres, passing more pillboxes until a fence appears on the left. (Three paths all go the same way but the highest is best.) Keep on and pass pillboxes. When fence bends sharp left downhill, keep on over the hump and down to the road at the next pillbox (113487). Cross and go up left. Left again, where track swings right up to another pillbox, and go straight on at the next pillbox.

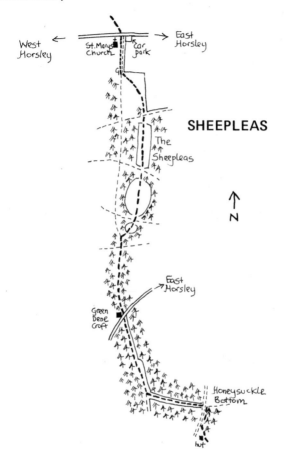

Pass two more pillboxes, one on left and one on right.
Swing up right with old wire fence on left. After 250 metres,
just after green space and where a path goes left, go right
through scrub and then left at a fork. (If you miss this turn go
right at the next cross tracks and pass a log seat on left.) Keep
on till you reach a wide track at the junction of six paths—

'Blindoak Gate'. Left for 20 metres, then right down a narrow
path through young trees. In 500 metres come to a foresters'
lean-to (093500). Fork right, then bear right on to a metalled
track and through a gate to Honeysuckle Bottom. Here go left
up a steep stony path and right at T-junction at the top. Later
cross a road opposite Green Dene Croft, and on up a
bridleway, which can be very muddy. Over a cross tracks, into
Sheepleas. Fork right to an open area in 30 metres, then left
and keep on, ignoring Bridleway sign, through glades, passing
several horse barriers, and join track at gate. Continue on
track at left of field to road at St Mary's Church, Horsley
(088526). If you went wrong on the many paths through
Sheepleas, make your way along the road to here.

Cross A246, through swing-gate and follow fence on right
till you are in the last field before railway, left by stile in left
hedge and then keep hedge on right to the road (200 metres
left on road is the Barley Mow). Go right on road 200 metres
to railway, where right on tarmac path with the line on the
left. Left at road junction and Horsley station is almost
directly opposite.

Information

Distance	9 miles. Map 187.	
Stations	Boxhill: half-hourly to Victoria or Waterloo.	
	Dorking: half-hourly.	
	Horsley: half-hourly, Sundays hourly, to Waterloo.	
	Gomshall: hourly, Sundays two-hourly.	
Buses	London Country 470 and Green Line 714. Leatherhead to Dorking, all hourly. London Country 408 Leatherhead to Guildford, on the A246 hourly.	
Admission	Polesden Lacey (National Trust). Garden open daily all year. House: April–October, Tuesday, Wednesday, Thursday, Saturday, Sunday, 2–6; March and November, weekends 2–5.	

Refreshments   Fort Tea Rooms, Boxhill summit; tea bar
Car park (171520). Burford Bridge
Hotel (172520), Barley Mow (W. Horsley),
Horsley Hotel Steak House (E. Horsley).
Nearest to middle of route is Ranmore
Arms (113502).

Accommodation   Tanners Hatch Youth Hostel; Dorking;
Gomshall; Guildford; Horsley.

The second stage gives quite a contrast to the first, less wild and with few hills. It has some beautiful footpaths, large stretches of wooded common and a mile of the Wey towpath. It shows the variety of Surrey's scenery, that we can have two such different, yet equally fine, walks next to each other. Soon after the start we go just by the edge of a new golf course in Barnsthorns Wood. This path has caused much work for the Ramblers' Association to preserve it. Before the golf course was started, the original path was a well-used one called the Blue Ride, which went in a straight line. When the golf course was proposed, to keep the path off the greens, the start was diverted to the edge of the wood, on condition that it was well marked and surfaced. However, despite many complaints, it was only after threats that the original path would be reinstated that work was done on the new route! If you follow the route in spring, you will see a mass of bluebells along it and will agree that the fuss was worth while. The woods are fairly open and make a popular walk for the people of Horsley.

After this path, we go along another, running along the edge of a slight ridge, and with a row of trees running either side, making the walk like a shaded avenue. There are splendid views on the right to the line of the North Downs where you should be able to pick out the route of the previous stage on the tops. It is deep remote countryside with the view only spoiled by a slight glimpse of the golf course. Further on we pass the tiny hamlets of May's Green and of Martyr's Green. Just on the left of the route is the Black Swan, a favourite pub for ramblers, which has been featured in two or three films.

About half a mile further away at Bridge End is another hotel, the Hautboy Inn. The Hautboy has an expensive but good restaurant on the ground floor, but serves cheaper food downstairs in the Spanish bar; around the back, up some stone steps, is the public bar in an astonishing large hall on the first floor. This is an enormous place, rather chilly in winter which must be seen to be appreciated—it caters for

quite a different clientele from the restaurant.

Past Martyr's Green, we have good views of an airfield on the left, looking trim and neat. It was proposed that a free pop festival should be held here, but this was not greeted with favour locally. Originally, the airfield was used by the British Aircraft Corporation for testing purposes, and the several footpaths across it were extinguished. The airfield was given up by B.A.C. some years ago and is now disused, but there is no sign of the paths being reinstated.

Continuing on this path we go into Ockham Common. This is a heavily wooded place, particularly near the beginning, and the rhododendrons are almost impenetrable. Just a bit off our route, on the right and hard to find despite its height, is Telegraph Hill with an old telegraph tower on it. This was one of a line built after the Napoleonic wars to connect London to Portsmouth—it was said that a message could go the whole distance in five minutes. This tower is the only five-storey one still standing, and linked Pewley Hill, in Guildford, with Claygate, near Kingston-on-Thames. You cannot get into the tower, but it is worth seeing; it is in a good glade for a picnic.

Ockham Common and its neighbour, Wisley Common across the A3, are in the hands of Surrey County Council and are good places to walk, ride, laze and also to collect eating chestnuts. Unfortunately, the M25 is going to come across here and destroy a good part of the woodland. Just before the A3, on the other side of a minor road, is Bolder Mere, a wide shallow expanse of water, which freezes over fairly readily and provides excellent skating. In summer, with an occasional fishing boat on it, it makes a good picture. The A3 is a wide dual carriageway and is hard to cross; a Green Line bus runs along it to London.

Wisley Common is much less wooded, but the multiplicity of paths still makes it difficult to navigate. You should come out directly opposite the entrance to the Royal Horticultural Society Gardens at Wisley. Here, the route goes on an enclosed path through the gardens with a view of lawns and trees, but the gardens proper cannot be seen from the path.

Telegraph Tower, Ockham Common

These are worth visiting at any time of the year. There are 200 acres altogether, with formal gardens, wild gardens, gardens around pools, and stretches of lawn and the natural Surrey woodland. As befits the headquarters of the Horticultural Society, the flowers are of all kinds providing a mass of colour, and labelled so that the keen gardener can rush off and try to reproduce the effects. Even in mid-winter the beautiful trees and lawns make it a pleasure to stroll here. At the right time of the year, surplus fruit is sold off cheaply— though there is normally a long queue.

After the gardens we come to Ockham Mill, a fine-looking place. Another good spot, now that it is bypassed, is Ripley, about 800 metres away. This has a number of pubs which provide good meals. Further on the route we have a mile walking by the Wey Navigation. This is a very old canal and was built soon after an Act of Parliament was passed in 1651. About 10 miles of canal were built where the river Wey was unsuitable for navigation, to allow barges to go from the Thames to Guildford. In 1760, a further 4 miles were authorized to extend the route to Godalming. The Navigation

continued in business until the 1960s, with the last horse-drawn barge being used in 1961. The canal was given to the National Trust in 1964 and is now deservedly popular with pleasure craft. It is 19½ miles long and runs from Weybridge to Godalming. It makes a good walk, with one of the best stretches being upstream from Ockham Mill to Pyrford.

Our own stretch is still a good one, with alders lining the banks and the Anchor, a good pub for a stop. 400 metres from this pub is Wisley Church, built about 1150 and worth looking at.

Route

From Horsley station, down Station Approach to the road (B2039) where turn right. 500 metres on, opposite East Lane, right at minor cross roads. 150 metres on, left by footpath sign. Follow near fence for 200 metres, then bear right and in 150 metres reach a footpath, the Blue Ride, through the woods. Left along this to a track after 800 metres. Right on track, and after 200 metres at top of rise, fork right. Follow avenue of trees to a wood, where right and follow the wood around edge of a field, with wood on left, to a stile in corner. Over stile and footbridge and on up to road (097565).

Left along road and, after 800 metres, right down a lane at May's Green. 100 metres on, left over a fence into a garden, by a footpath sign. Over stile at rear and left of house. Keep fence on left then quarter-left across field and on up a track. When it swings left, keep on along path between fences. Left at road (500 metres left is the Black Swan). Right after 100 metres by bridleway sign. At end, left at staggered cross tracks (ignore bridleway sign). Soon pass house on right. Later fork left 20 metres after horse barrier. Right at track (house on left). Left 80 metres after field ends, past seat. 200 metres on, right—at U-shaped tree—then left on to firebreak. Soon right into car park. Cross and right on to road. Keep on to A3 (078586). Public convenience on right open 7.30 a.m. to sunset, with water tap inside.

Cross A3, carefully! 40 metres up track, at cross tracks, 'No Horses' sign, go left and uphill. Pass to right of house, then

Bolder Mere, by the A3

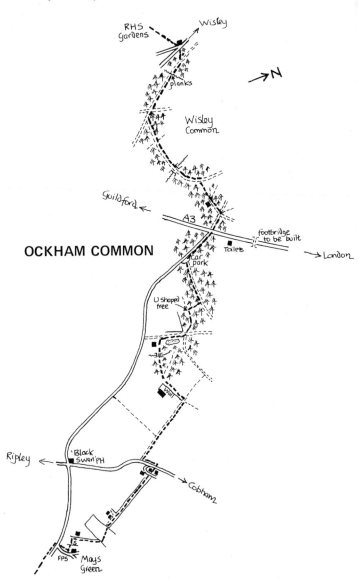

straight on downhill. Left at bottom on a wide firebreak. Over
footbridge and keeping a little left, go straight on at
cross tracks. Right at T-junction. Keep on over cross tracks.
250 metres after planks over stream, bear left to road, where
road splits (065588). Over stile to left of house and on
enclosed path through R.H.S. Garden. At end, over stile into
a field. Cross to next stile and over second field. Pass houses
on right and right on lane. Pass Ockham Mill, over stream
and follow track right. Cross two stiles and on to River Wey.
Cross footbridge and on to next stretch of water, the canal.
Right, and follow towpath for $1\frac{1}{4}$ miles. Pass the Anchor and,
800 metres after, left over next bridge and follow track
between hedgerows. Cross last field to end of pylons, and at
road right 600 metres to cross A245 at lights, down Station
Approach and under the subway to West Byfleet station.

Information

Distance	$8\frac{1}{2}$ miles; total $17\frac{1}{2}$. Maps 187 and 1 mile on 186.
Stations	Horsley: half-hourly, Sundays hourly. West Byfleet: half-hourly, to Waterloo.
Buses	Green Line 715, London to Guildford on A3.
Admission	R.H.S. Gardens, Wisley. Open all year, weekdays 10–7, or sunset. Sundays 2–7, or sunset.
Refreshments	Black Swan (089572), car park (078588), R.H.S. Gardens, Anchor (053593).
Accommodation	Difficult on route. Guildford, West Byfleet, Woking.

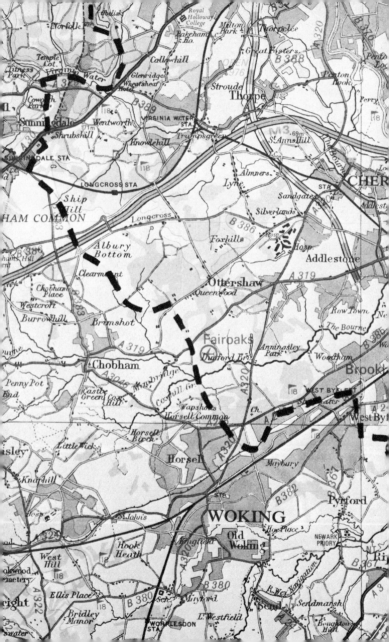

Apart from the first 2 miles by the old Basingstoke canal, this stage is almost all across two large commons, Horsell Common and the wilder and barer Chobham Common.

As so many canals do, the Basingstoke canal allows us to escape from urban surroundings into a different, green world. The canal was opened to traffic in 1794 and, in a fit of patriotic enthusiasm, the owners waived tolls for the Napoleonic wars. Unfortunately, this was the only time the canal ever did any real business and there was a steady decline from then on, with the original company going into liquidation in 1866. The canal has had a whole succession of different owners since then, each of whom has tried to do something with it, but none succeeded. The last barge went up to Basingstoke in 1914 and the last to Woking in 1949. It is now owned jointly by Hampshire and Surrey County Councils and it is planned to restore it by voluntary labour.

The canal used to run from its junction with the Wey at Byfleet to Basingstoke, a distance of 40 miles, but the route only now exists up to the Greywell tunnel entrance, near Hook, leaving 28 miles to be opened up. The towpath can be walked the whole way, but only a few stretches are navigable. Our 2 miles certainly are not! It has a decaying charm about it, though, with the gardens leading down to the channel, the birds in the woods nearby and the rushes and flowers in the canal bed. There was one surrealist scene in the Spring, with water lilies, swans, rusted bikes and oil drums all together on one shallow patch of water.

We leave the canal only about 800 metres from the centre of Woking. This is a new, rather characterless town that grew up round the railway station. It has had neither the advantages of a natural growth and old buildings nor those of the planned new towns with a coherent structure. However, some efforts are being made to improve it, with a well-laid out new pedestrian shopping area. There is also the Shah Jehan Mosque.

However, Woking is surrounded by heathland and we can go from the canal, straight on to Horsell Common. It is rather littered just by the road, but very soon we are treading on pine needles and going on a good path through the trees at the beginning of the common. The trees change from conifers to birches and then gradually fade out, before we come to a path which eventually goes by the side of Fairoaks aerodrome.

This is a pleasant airfield with grass runways, and the aircraft take off and land right over the path, sometimes only feet away. There is a proposal to have concrete runways, but this is being fiercely contested.

Opposite the end of the aerodrome there are some old sheds where Ministry of Defence records were evacuated during the war. We pass these, go into woods again and then, just before the road, pass a delightfully situated house in the trees. After this road, we have a good country path, passing a wood on the left where I always seem to see someone sawing up logs, over a stream and then by the end of a fine-looking garden to come out on a road just before Chobham common. Left 1,000 metres down the road is Burrowhill with two pubs, the only refreshment places near the route.

Chobham Common, sometimes called the Wastes, is a very large common, mostly bare of trees, and gives a sensation of open moorland more usually associated with the North of England. The majority of it is owned by Surrey County Council and, at 1,400 acres, is the council's largest open space. It is well used by horses as well as walkers and some of the paths can be very muddy. Schemes are being considered to try to separate users to make paths better underfoot for walkers. Despite all these users, it can still seem a lonely place in the middle of the common, with not a house to be seen.

On the left, going across the common, is a little wooded hill, Staple Hill. On top of this there used to be a ring of trees, Chobham Clump, standing like a miniature Chanctonbury Ring. But, one night, when there were six trees, someone came out with a chain-saw and cut them down—what a pity it is so easy to destroy what takes so long to grow. The view from the hill is still good but the best direction is spoilt by the new M3 motorway. Fortunately, it is not too obtrusive elsewhere, and

Basingstoke Canal, Woking

it does not take away that desolate feeling that the common can give. There is a tunnel underneath the road for walkers, and mounting blocks thoughtfully placed on each side for horse riders.

On the other side, the path goes across an area which was badly affected by fire during 1976's hot summer. The heather was almost burnt out between the motorway and the next little road; you could use this piece to measure the recuperative powers of heather. A stone pillar on a small hill ahead acts as a guidepost for use. It is 4 metres high and was erected in 1901 to commemorate the occasion in 1853 when Queen Victoria reviewed eight thousand of her troops before they set out for the Crimea. Looking from here to the right, we can see standing out on a rise a number of large prosperous-looking houses surrounded by greenery. This is Sunningdale and the famous Wentworth golf course, scene of

many top class events. Our route keeps on the common to come out at a humbler area of Sunningdale, near the railway station: there are shops, pubs, a Chinese restaurant, and a good train service to Staines and London.

Route

From West Byfleet station, opposite end of subway, go under railings, and quarter-left across grass to road bend. Keep on to car park and on up path to Basingstoke Canal. Left along towpath for 2 miles to second bridge where right on road.

After 150 metres and after pylon go left into woods. Path exits from wood, when cross road and continue along a rough road, Carlton road. Cross two more roads and on to Horsell Common (010603).

Keep on for 1,200 metres in same direction (320°), taking the left fork when in doubt, to far side, where left at track T-junction. Right after 12 metres, by Young Stroat Farm, and follow path and fence on left to gate, opposite house on right.

Left into field and follow fence on right. Over two footbridges and a gate. Fairoaks Aerodrome is on right. Right at A319 for 90 metres, then left up drive. Around left bend and opposite end house on left, bear right up path. Bear left at top and keep on, passing house on left to road (997633). Left along road for 400 metres, then right at bend in the road. 60 metres in, left over stile and along path beside field. Over stile at end into field. Cross until 20 metres before stile on far side, where right and follow fence on left. Over next stile and half-left to footbridge (989632). Cross and over stile. Ahead over field (310°) to far left corner and over stile. Follow track ahead over grid, to road. (Left 1,200 metres down road for Burrowhill and pubs.)

Cross and up track opposite. 80 metres on, bear right on to Chobham Common proper. Left at cross tracks 150 metres on, right fork, then left 300 metres on at next cross tracks and under pylons. Ahead to wooded ridge, where bear right over road to Staple Hill (971646). Left (290°) down to tunnel under M3.

Out of tunnel half-right 100 metres to fire signpost, then

Horsell Common, Woking

half-left (340°) and keep ahead. Cross road and over ridge to
right of memorial column. Later swing left by railway to road,
where right and over bridge (958666). (Carry on for 400
metres to A30, then left and in 300 metres reach Sunningdale
station.) Walk continues 40 metres on right into Onslow road.

Information

Distance	9 miles; total 26½. Maps 175 and 4 miles 186.
Stations	West Byfleet: half-hourly to Waterloo. Sunningdale: half-hourly, hourly Sundays to Waterloo.
Refreshments	None in middle, nearest is Red Lion at Burrowhill (973629). Pubs and Chinese restaurant at Sunningdale.
Accommodation	Very difficult. Ascot, Staines.

Queen Victoria Memorial, Chobham Common

This stage is a splendid walk through the length of Windsor Park, finishing by Windsor castle. It goes almost entirely through open land but, in contrast to the last section with its commons, it is parkland, tamed and designed for private and now public enjoyment. But very good parkland it is, and if you want to be away from the crowds you can still manage it—if you avoid Sunday afternoons in summer. We leave Surrey on this stage and enter Berkshire.

The walk starts at Sunningdale through some pleasant housing in Shrubs Hill and, after crossing the busy A30, passes the Red Lion. This is early to stop if you are doing one stage but is a good lunch break if you are doing two. It is an ordinary workaday pub with a good public bar, no carpets, some food and plenty of room. Going by a path at the side of this, we go through Coworth Park, which is now farmland containing a stud farm and some fine horses to look at.

The rest of the walk is in Windsor Great Park. This is not open as of right to the public and there are no public footpaths, but the public is allowed to wander through almost the whole area at will. However, it is only open during daylight hours so in winter make an early start! There are many possible different routes through the park and the Countryway uses just one. It takes in many of the park's best features but still leaves out both the Valley gardens and the Savill gardens. To fit these in as well would make a very full day—come back again for them.

The route starts by going by the southern shore of Virginia Water. On an autumn or winter morning with few people about, it makes a good imitation of a Scottish loch. It is an artificial lake and was created by the Duke of Cumberland, 'the Butcher of Culloden', in the eighteenth century. He was forest ranger of the park for twenty years, did a lot to improve it and a little to pay back for his army's conduct in the Highlands after Culloden. The lake is a conspicuous landmark and was drained in the Second World War to hinder German bombers' air navigation.

After about a mile walking by the lake, we pass some ruins that look rather non-Scottish. These are Roman ruins brought from Leptis Magna in Libya and re-erected in 1827 by George IV's architect Sir Jeffry Wyattville. A little later on, there are some waterfalls on the left, designed to fit the Scottish atmosphere; they use boulders brought from Bagshot Heath and, to me, look much more like Bagshot than Braemar! On the other side of the lake, we pass an intricately carved totem pole. This is 100 feet (30 metres) high to symbolize the centenary of British Columbia and was given by the Indians of Vancouver Island. Despite its height it is well hidden in the trees and if you take the wrong turning is easily missed.

We then go by Smith's Lawn, which is a polo ground now, though in the last war it was an airfield—we need to make a diversion if polo is being played. The statue on the left is of the Prince Consort and is not the Copper Horse. It is after passing Cumberland Lodge that we come to the famous statue of George III, erected in 1831—the Copper Horse. It is of considerable size, and after building it the workmen had a sit down lunch inside it. From the base of the statue, we have a superb view down the 3-mile Long Walk to Windsor Castle. This is shaded by the trees planted in 1945 which in turn replaced the original elms planted by Charles II in 1685.

The Long Walk seems an apt name when doing it, as Windsor Castle seems to take a long time in getting near. Despite the royal nature of the walk, there is a big obstacle at the end in the lack of a zebra crossing for the A308. There is a final walk through the Home Park to the edge of the castle and then into Windsor High Street.

There is so much to see in Windsor that a rest day is indicated to look round it. If you haven't time for that, try to spend an afternoon here. Windsor Castle is a 'must', with its state apartments, tower, St George's Chapel and the Queen's paintings and, most of all, its history. A good guide book is available in Windsor Castle and only the most important historical points are mentioned here.

A Castle was first built at Windsor in 1070 by William the Conqueror, to guard the Thames Valley. It was on the

Copper Horse Statue, Windsor Park

present site and about its current size but was made of earth and wood. Henry II built the Round Tower and had the outer castle walls built in stone. The magnificent St George's Chapel was started by Edward IV in about 1480. Parliamentary forces held the town and castle in the civil war; Charles I was imprisoned here for a time and in 1649 his body was buried in St George's Chapel.

After the Civil War, Charles II had the present range of state apartments built by Hugh May and had the Long Walk laid out. The Castle was then rather neglected until George IV had Sir Jeffry Wyattville make it a comfortable living place instead of a castle. He added new towers, extended the Long Walk and doubled the height of the Round Tower. Little major work has been done since, but Queen Victoria had various statues and a mausoleum built.

The tour of the castle starts with the King Henry VIII Gateway. This has the arms of Henry VIII and Catherine of Aragon, his first wife, above and leads into the lower ward. On the left is the Guard Room with Garter Tower and Salisbury Tower on either side, circular towers built by Henry VIII. The Curfew Tower on the NW corner of the castle, used to be a prison and now contains the chapel bells; by this is the Library Terrace which gives a good view of the Thames Valley and the Chilterns. Directly opposite the gateway is St George's Chapel.

This is a magnificently decorated, light and airy perpendicular church giving a tremendous feeling of space. It was originally built between 1480 and 1530, and was restored in the 1920s, so that it looks fresh and clean. The whole nave is covered by rich vaulting, with many carved bosses. These include St George's cross, Henry VIII's arms and many repeats of a hemp-bray. A mirror is provided so that the details may be seen better. The west window is of sixteenth-century stained glass, contains seventy-five figures of kings, saints, and popes, and makes a marvellous sight. Not quite so impressive is the white marble monument to Princess Charlotte, daughter of King George IV.

The choir is altogether different, with dark sombre wood and is richly magnificent throughout. It contains the stalls for the members of the Order of the Garter. Above each knight's stall hangs his banner with his coat of arms, and in each are enamelled shields, displaying the arms of all the knights who have ever had that stall. There are now over seven hundred of these shields dating back to the fourteenth century. The whole panoply makes a brilliant sight. There are carved figures almost everywhere, with carvings under the seats of biblical scenes, St George and some animals. One has a monkey giving medicine to a dog. In the middle of the choir floor is a vault which contains the bodies of Henry VIII, Jane Seymour, his second wife, and King Charles 1. On the left of the high altar is the tomb of Edward IV with a pair of beautifully delicate iron gates, made by John Tresilian in about 1482. Outside is the 2-metres polished sword of Edward III, with a painting next to it showing him holding the sword.

The Albert Memorial Chapel is near to St George's Chapel, and is worthwhile seeing for its Victorian decoration—a memorial by Queen Victoria for Prince Albert.

The middle ward of the castle has the Round Tower, 30 metres in diameter. The top—65 metres above the Thames— gives a splendid view of the country from the Chilterns to the North Downs. The Royal Standard is flown from the flag post when the Queen is in residence.

In the upper ward are the state apartments, open when the Court is not in residence. These are the original apartments built for Charles II and Catharine of Braganza, and were built by Hugh May in the 1670s. The carvings by Grinling Gibbons and the ceilings by Verrio are the most interesting features; but the bed of Empress Eugénie (wife of Napoleon III) and the sword surrendered to Lord Louis Mountbatten on the Japanese surrender in 1945 are worth seeing. The apartments themselves are of a grandeur to suit visiting royalty, with the Garter Throne Room and the Grand Reception Room especially so. However, the chief reason to visit these is to see the paintings hung in the apartments. There are Van Dycks, Holbeins, Rubens, Rembrandts, Canalettos, and more besides. Note particularly Van Dyck's portraits of King Charles I and of his children; Rubens's Holy Family, and a self portrait; and Rembrandt's portrait of his mother.

The paintings in the rooms are often lent to other galleries, but there is such richness available that this should not affect the visit. In the hall by the entrance to the apartments is a separate collection of Old Master drawings, including the Leonardo da Vinci sketches and some of the finest of Holbein's drawings.

Of a rather different character is the Queen's Doll's House, given to Queen Mary in 1923 as a symbol of good will. It was designed by Sir Edwin Lutyens, and is on a scale of 1:12. The house is $2\frac{1}{2}$ metres by $1\frac{1}{2}$ metres, so it represents a fair sized real house! It has a grand staircase, a dining room with places set for 14 people, a garage with 1920s cars and a luggage room. Perhaps what shows the 1920s best, though, are the antiquated bath rooms. This exhibition can be very crowded and is more for adults than for children.

You will find it rather expensive if you try to see everything there is to see and, if you do, you will probably be more tired than walking a whole stage, so leave plenty of time for it. Windsor provides a good variety of refreshment places to rest

your weary feet in—however, do keep a look out for one or two people charging well over a proper price to tourists who, they think, will not know any better.

Route

From Sunningdale station, left along A30 for 300 metres, then right and in 400 metres reach Onslow Road (958666) for start of route. Left along this, left on path in circle at end, right in 50 metres and keep on path to join Shrubs Hill Lane. Keep on to A30. Right for 200 metres to Red Lion, then left by bridleway at the side of the pub, through Coworth Park. Keep on to A329. Left for 150 metres, then right into car park. Through gate opposite into Windsor Great Park. (Open daylight only.)

Ahead to lake, where right and follow edge for 2 miles to Totem Pole (980695) 30 metres high. Take first right signed to Savill Gardens, and at next signpost veer left to Smiths Lawn. Go up to right of buildings and keep ahead along right edge of polo field. The obelisk can be seen in the trees on the right. Go right when grassland extends to right and pass green horse stalls on right. There are water taps here. At slight bend go half-left (360°) to Cumberland Gate.

Through gate and half-left (340°) through trees. Pass tennis court and on for 200 metres to fence. Left along fence to pond on left, then follow wide track ahead and up between field hedges to the Copper Horse statue. A splendid view from the top! Over the hill and on down the Long Walk (3 miles) and over A308 to Windsor Castle.

Bear left at end through gate into Park Street. Right at end into Windsor High Street. Pass castle on right to bridge over River Thames. Continue on the right to Riverside station for Waterloo.

Windsor Bridge and Windsor Castle

Information

Distance 9 miles; total 35½ miles. Map 175.

Stations Sunningdale: half-hourly, hourly Sundays.
Windsor Riverside: half-hourly to
Waterloo. Windsor Central: half-hourly to
Slough and then Paddington. Does not run
on winter Sundays.

Buses Englefield Green: Green Line 701 Ascot to
London; 718 Windsor to London; 725
Gravesend to Windsor—all hourly.
Windsor: Green Line 704, 705 to London.
London Country 353 to Ashley Green
hourly, two-hourly on Sundays. London
Country 441 to High Wycombe hourly.

Admission Savill Gardens, March to October 10 a.m.
–6 p.m. Windsor Castle precincts free.
10 a.m.–4 p.m., or 1 hour before sunset,
whichever is later. State apartments,
Queen Mary's Dolls' House, Old
Master drawings—all open March to
October, 10.30 a.m.–5 p.m. weekdays and
1.30 p.m.–5 p.m. Sundays. November to
February 10.30 a.m.–3 p.m. weekdays, no
Sundays. State apartments not open when
Queen is in residence. St George's Chapel
Mondays to Saturdays 11 a.m.–3.45
p.m., Friday 1 p.m.–3.45 p.m., Sundays
2.15 p.m.–3.45 p.m. Additionally open free
for church services.

Refreshments Red Lion at Sunningdale; Sun at Englefield
Green; good restaurant *inside* Savill
Gardens; numerous pubs, cafés and
restaurants at Windsor.

Accommodation Windsor Youth Hostel; Windsor;
Maidenhead.

This stage shows the Thames at its most popular, with launches galore, fishermen, and those places—Maidenhead and Marlow—which bring back the novels of the twenties and thirties. The route starts at Windsor bridge, which used to be a main traffic route before the Windsor bypass was built. Now it is restricted to foot traffic only, but is still crowded in summer with tourists making their way between Eton and Windsor. Eton College is at the end of Eton High Street, and it is worth diverting to inspect the buildings where so many of our past and present rulers received their education.

It was founded by Henry VI in 1440 and provided for a provost, ten secular priests, seventy scholars, a school master, sixteen choristers and thirteen poor infirm men. Gradually, however, all the revenues went to the school, and the 'poor scholars' in turn became the sons of the richest in the kingdom. Entering School Yard from the Lime Walk, the chapel is seen on the right. Henry VI intended it to be twice as long, but it is still of a size and splendour to compare with King's College, Cambridge, or St George's Chapel in Windsor. On the walls are a series of wall paintings, dating from the late fifteenth century, whitewashed and hidden for centuries, but now, a little dimmed, revealed for all to see again. Lower School, opposite the chapel, is the original schoolroom, used continuously since about 1445.

The walk itself goes along the north bank of the Thames for about 7 miles. At the start it goes by Brocas, a riverside meadow owned by Eton, and passes Eton School boathouses. The river is fascinating, particularly the river traffic with those beautiful young women displayed on the tops of the pleasure craft—be careful not to fall in watching them, and do not trip over the fishermen who abound on the bank at all hours. About $1\frac{1}{2}$ miles from the start a small church is passed standing among elms just off the river bank. Boveney church is of twelfth-century origin but is unfortunately kept locked. After a further $1\frac{1}{2}$ miles, we pass Oakley Court on the other side. This is a large turreted house, where Hammer films made their earlier horror films, including the Dracula ones. On the right, a little further on is Dorney church, worth making the 400 metres detour from the river to see—a pub is on the main road (B3026) just beyond it. I made my first visit to it by accident, seeking shelter and safety from a violent thunderstorm throwing lightning at the river. It was about one in the morning and this little church was most impressive in the torchlight, with its rows of pews giving it a very Georgian look. A return visit showed the fifteenth-century woodwork, the wall paintings, and the splendid musicians gallery (1630). Dorney Court next door is not open to the public, but is a fine fifteenth-century timber framed building.

Returning to the river, we go under the M4 motorway bridge and pass the village and church of Bray on the other side of the river. Bray is famous for its Vicar, but his career is difficult to identify with the legend.

The river bank here has those river-fronted houses with the film star look, bringing back the reputation of Maidenhead as the 'naughty' place of the 1920s, the place where the fast set came for a spin out of town. By Maidenhead bridge, built in 1777, we pass Skindles, another atmospheric hotel—this time of the Guards and the Edwardian era. Bulldog Drummond, that rather faded and distant hero, used to eat here. The town itself does not live up to this expectation, but does offer a good deal of necessary convenience in its restaurants of diverse types, shops and a launderette.

Just past the bridge and the Riviera Inn, there is a little lane on the left leading to the Reitlinger museum. In a typical Edwardian riverside house, the museum contains a wide selection of Chinese, Persian, Peruvian and European pottery, as well as African and European glass and sculpture, but, due to its only being open mid-week, I have not personally been able to check its interest.

The walk goes along the other side of the river, for a short period, to Boulter's Lock. This is a very popular spot with the bridge crowded with people watching the equally crowded boats go through the locks. Don't pass by, but go over the bridge, past the Boulter's Lock Inn, and refreshment stall, to

Boulter's Lock, Maidenhead
Ray Mill Island, Maidenhead

go over a little bridge to Ray Mill Island. This is a delightful little public park, next to the Thames, with a few gardens, a streamlet, and pleasant lawns to picnic on. It is a good halfway point for this stage of the walk. The island also has a public putting green and, most unusually, a public croquet lawn. If you are a croquet addict, like me, you may find it difficult to move on. But there is still lots to see, so try to make the effort, or else split this section into two and return from Maidenhead.

From Boulter's Lock, the journey could be continued by the towpath, but we cut inland for a change. After going past some gravel workings, where the path has been diverted, the route goes past an intriguing channel of water called Strand Water and then comes out at Cookham Moor, by a green.

Directly opposite is a pub, the Crown, and the route continues on the left of it. However, before continuing, be

sure to go into the centre of Cookham and visit the Stanley Spencer Gallery. This is a small art museum devoted to Stanley Spencer, one of the most original artists Britain has produced. He lived most of his life in the Cookham area, and many of his pictures are set here. The museum is small, homely and welcoming. There are some mementoes of Stanley Spencer and about fifty of his paintings, most of them set in and around Cookham. They also include some of his paintings about shipbuilding on the Clyde done during the last War. The paintings are full of large moon-faced people, Spencer's trademark. They are not to everyone's taste, but in my opinion they fit well with his themes. There are a number of paintings of scenes around Cookham, particularly of the river. His last, and unfinished painting, 'Christ preaching at Cookham regatta', is there. It is a large painting, 5 metres by 2 metres, and the impression it makes is enhanced in some way by its unfinished state. The scene is by the Ferry Hotel at Cookham, and shows crowds of people enjoying themselves in and around boats and only giving half their attention to Christ preaching. The unaccustomed familiarity of the setting brings out the likely reality far more than the traditional remote settings.

A little further on past the gallery is Cookham church, where Spencer's famous painting, the 'Last Supper', hangs, though it is often out on loan. The church is twelfth century and is well worth visiting. Inside the porch is seen one of the massive masonry walls of the original Norman church.

A final worthwhile diversion from the route goes by footpath from the churchyard to the river and the Ferry Inn. This is a large boisterous place with several bars, good bar-snacks, and Truman's ales. It is a popular place, but spacious, with fine views from the lawns, where you can imagine Stanley Spencer's scenes. Walk back to the route on the road. Notice a small fading notice on Vine Cottage, next to the Bel and Dragon, telling you that 'All fighting must cease by 10 o'clock.' The pub is fifteenth century, and serves Young's ales and does good home-made soup. There are other old houses, pubs and cafés on the road back.

Moor Hall, Cookham

The Countryway continues across Cookham Moor
(National Trust) and by the side of Cock Marsh, also owned
by the N.T. and an excellent spot for marshland birds.
Further on, the route comes to Winter Hill: this is a good
viewpoint with views across the river of the Chiltern hills, and
a patchwork of green and brown fields. The gravel pits are
used for water-skiing. Ignore the small sewage works, the view
is on the right! This section finishes on a beautiful path
through Quarry Woods and by Marlow bridge to Marlow.

A bridge has existed at Marlow since the fourteenth
century, with the present bridge designed by William Tierney
Clark and built in 1832. On this side of the bridge is the
Compleat Angler, and on the other side, Marlow parish
church, modern and spacious. Marlow is a pleasant place, but
one does have to look for the places of interest. Marlow Place,
in Station Road, was built by Thomas Archer in 1720, and
there are several good Georgian houses in West Street and the
High Street. Behind the church, off a little passageway to the
right, is St Peter's Street with the old parsonage and deanery
that can be peeped at. The High Street has a milestone in it
for the 'Hatfield to Reading turnpike', an unusual main road:
it was built and signposted by the Cecil family in the 1820s to
ease the journey from Hatfield to the waters at Bath. For
finishers at Marlow, there is a railway station (closed on
Sundays) and a bus service to High Wycombe or
Maidenhead.

Route

From Windsor Riverside station, right, then at river left along
towpath. Right after 80 metres, over pedestrian bridge. At far
side left along Brocas Street, soon forking left past
Waterman's Arms, then ahead and through gate to towpath.
1,200 metres on, ahead under bridge carrying the A332. (For
youth hostel: climb steps on right, then cross bridge and road,
then down slip road and right twice.) 40 metres after bridge,
bear right (350°) across field to re-meet river at footbridge at
river bend. Follow towpath for $6\frac{3}{4}$ miles altogether, to

'Christ Preaching At Cookham Regatta' by Stanley Spencer
View from Winter Hill

Maidenhead at the third road bridge (902813).

Left over bridge (for bus station, continue till roundabout, then left—right after this for railway station), then right along road beside river for 500 metres till reach Boulter's Inn at lock. Left down Ray Mill Road East. After 400 metres, just after the Pagoda, right down short enclosed footpath and along Summerleaze road opposite. When road turns left, right 15 metres and left along rough track 350 metres to its end. Left at footpath sign over stile, over one bridge, and then in 100 metres, right over second bridge over Maidenhead ditch. Take right hand path of two to stile, cross gravel track and slightly right across next field to gravel track again. Right 200 metres, then left over stile and ahead with fence on right. Over stile in corner, over stream and then half turn left to follow

hedge to far left corner. Over stile and along path by iron fence. At end, before bridge, right with Strand Water on left, and follow left edge of field. Half turn right at end by stile, and then by iron fence and on enclosed path coming out by Moor Hall on road opposite Cookham Moor (893854).

Ahead across moor and roads, with Crown Inn on right, to field gate and N.T. sign to Cockmarsh. Half turn left to middle stile of three (350°), diagonally ahead across next field to stile and then a second stile. Cross then right along an overgrown path by the edge of a small sewage works. 200 metres on, over stile and ahead along right edge of golf course. Leave course in far right corner, over stile and under bridge. Ahead along track (right) leading to N.T. area of Cockmarsh, bear left, and later climb gradually with fine views of Thames. Track comes out on road at Winter Hill Farm, where turn right then ahead across cross roads. Just before Dial Close Cottage, take right path through woods. Later fork right, then up to a road and, without crossing road, immediately down again by a steep, stepped path to a road corner. Continue right along the road to Marlow Bridge (851861).

Cross the Thames and pass the George and Dragon Hotel on right. (For Marlow station, take right turn on Station Road and reach Marlow station in 500 metres.) To continue route, take first left into Pound Lane. Pass toilets on left and then opposite car park, right along alley to road. Right for 20 metres then left into Quoitings Square and Oxford Road to pass the bus station.

Information

Distance	13 miles; total 48½ miles. Map 175.
Stations	Windsor: half-hourly to Waterloo. Maidenhead: half-hourly, hourly Sundays, to Paddington. Cookham and Marlow: hourly to Maidenhead, not Sundays.

Thames at Marlow

Buses	Alder 20/20A, 3 an hour Windsor, Maidenhead, Cookham, High Wycombe. 18, hourly, two-hourly Sundays, Marlow to Maidenhead. 28, 3 an hour, hourly Sundays, Marlow to High Wycombe.
Admission	Eton College Schoolyard and chapel, 2–5 p.m. daily. Henry Reitlinger museum at Maidenhead, Tues–Thurs, 10.00 a.m.–12.30 p.m. and 2.15–4.30 p.m. Apr–Sept. Free. Stanley Spencer Gallery at Cookham, April to October, daily 10.30 a.m.–1 p.m. and 2–6.30 p.m. Winter weekends only 11 a.m.–1 p.m. and 2–5 p.m.
Refreshments	Cafés and pubs at Maidenhead. Also refreshment stall before and at Boulter's Lock. Bel and Dragon, Ferry Inn and other pubs and a restaurant at Cookham.
Accommodation	Youth hostels at Windsor and Henley. Maidenhead, Marlow.

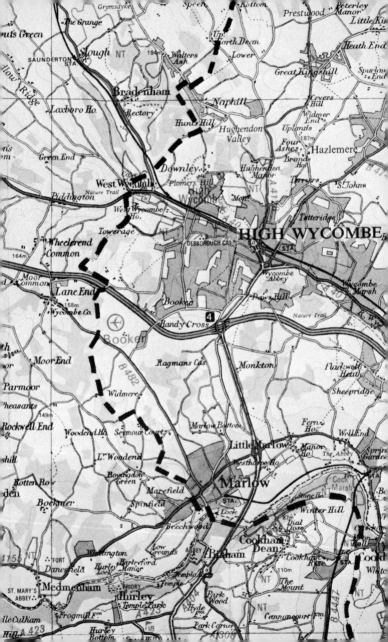

This stage marks the start of the Chilterns, which we will be walking through for the next four sections, or about 30 miles in all. It is an area of beechwoods and narrow valleys, with a multiplicity of footpaths. These used to be badly overgrown and under-used, but the efforts of the Chilterns Society and the Ramblers Association over the last few years have cleared and signposted them. They are now a pleasure to walk, and are therefore much more used than before. It can be strenuous country though, with many steep valleys to cross, so don't be ambitious with your daily mileage.

This section gives a gentle start to the area, with some climbs but not as steep as later. The initial walk out of Marlow has some good views of the Thames Valley behind, so stop and look backwards sometimes. In the distance you will see the North Downs where the route started. Blounts Wood offers a pleasant path, then there is a steep climb up to the road at Copy Farm. A little further on is Copy Green, a small green with about four cottages, and beyond that, by Widmore Farm, there is the remains of a thirteenth-century chapel, with an undercroft. A key can be obtained at the farm if you wish to look at the chapel.

Further on, after passing through Shillingridge wood, we come to an immaculately kept group of farm buildings, cottages and stables. This is Bluey's Farm. The cottages and stables are perfectly thatched and in excellent repair, with hanging baskets and a well, and trim hedges by the side of each. On the left is an older house with tiled roof, a wooden frame and cross-hatched brick-work, and on the right is a rock garden. It is beautiful, but has a strangely deserted air. Each visit I made I saw no one there and it seemed more and more unreal and dreamlike. After making several enquiries I solved the mystery. The farm is owned by a Greek ship-owner, Mr Mavroleon, and used only occasionally. Except for the old house, it was built about 1960, and was originally a stud-farm, though it is not used as such now. The sign seen hanging at the farm is an inn sign, as one of the houses has been recreated as a private inn, rather in the way that other people have cocktail cabinets. Knowledge has not altered my affection for the place, and it is still charming to linger here and imagine what it might have been like.

After Bluey's Farm, there is a walk along the bottom of a dry valley and then a satisfying mile along a track in Moor Wood. After a lane, we come to a second thick wood and pass a small waterworks at the top of the hill. The way out of this wood is by a narrow overgrown path, to come out by a motorway, the M40. We emerge from the enchanted forest to everyday life! We now get occasional glimpses of a shining ball in the distance: the 'golden ball' on the church at West Wycombe, where we are heading.

West Wycombe is full of places to see, and a half-day could be spent easily in seeing them. The village was bought from the owner, Sir John Dashwood, by the Royal Society of Arts in 1929. After a successful appeal for funds, the village was restored and handed to the National Trust in 1934. The

village fits together and it is the whole that makes the impact rather than the individual buildings—although the fifteenth-century church loft and village lock-up are worth a special look. The traffic on the A40 may make it a little hard to walk down the street admiring the overhanging storeys. The inns are worth a visit, too, and still take visitors at varying prices. The George and Dragon is an old coaching inn, with an alleged ghost who haunts the bar playing the fiddle—not fiddling the bar! At the rear there used to be a gallery where people could wait for the incoming stage-coaches, and there is now a large garden to sit in.

Opposite is the Plough Inn, another old inn, built on a slope and with its bar upstairs. At the back there is a little garden from which there is a very fine view of the village roofs, very revealing about a place. As well as antiquity, these pubs have the essential qualities of a good pub—a friendly atmosphere, good beer and food.

At the bottom of the hill leading to the caves, and very different from this domestic side of the village, is the entrance to West Wycombe House and its surrounding parkland, also owned by the National Trust. The house was built in its present form by the second Baronet, Sir Francis Dashwood, in the period 1745–71. The plans were made, and remade, by Sir Francis himself, who employed architects to carry out his ideas rather than their own. He changed his mind several times over the years, and there are some curious features because of this. The house and parkland give the impression of one man's ideas in his lifetime and are certainly not today's committee architecture. The designs for the house came from Francis Dashwood's many Grand Tours of Europe, particularly from Italy and the Near East.

The most famous external feature is the double colonnade at the rear, in a generalized Palladian style which gives it the remarkable look of a stage-set. The west of the house has a portico designed by Dashwood's chief architect, Revett, based on his drawings from the Near East. The interior is richly decorated and is a delight to walk through. The ceilings have designs or classical pictures, with the best known done by

Bluey's Farm nr Marlow

Guiseppe Borgnis. His 'Triumph of Bacchus and Ariadne' is richly coloured and blends with the flock wallpaper of the 'Blue' drawing room—the whole impression is of Italian opulence. Despite the different styles, it seems to me to fit together remarkably well. The house was designed to blend into the parkland, which is an example of a 'natural landscape' garden.

There is a lake, islands, a cascade, meandering walks, and many different buildings placed around the parkland. These include the temple of Apollo, the Round temple, the Music temple, and Daphne's temple, all classical but of different shapes. These have been restored by the National Trust to their previous eighteenth-century glory, but we have to imagine what it would have been like at the opening of the house with its grand fête, a warship on the lake, and Bacchanalian revels.

On the hill opposite, where the Countryway goes, are other creations of Sir Francis Dashwood. On the side of the hill, and going 400 metres into the hill are the Hell-Fire caves. These were excavated in the eighteenth century to provide materials for building a new road between West Wycombe and High Wycombe, a project to provide work for the relief of unemployment. (Perhaps we could do likewise today and derive use rather than waste from the talents and energy of the unemployed.) The caves get their name from the Hell-Fire Club of which Sir Francis was a member. Members took pseudonyms, so not all members are known even now, but the famous radical M.P. John Wilkes was one. Over the years stories were generated about the club holding 'nameless' orgies, but this doesn't seem to be true—it was an attempt to discredit reformers by blackening their names with irrelevancies! The caves are now lit, and there are models of figures in the alcoves and there is an underground stream, the Styx, that can be seen. Interesting, but rather over-priced.

On the top of the hill is the mausoleum and the church. The mausoleum was built in 1765 with £500 bequeathed by Lord Melcombe, a member of the Hell-Fire Club. It is an open

West Wycombe Village
Roofs of West Wycombe

hexagonal building with thick walls, each 20 metres in length, and has large columns and urns on each corner. It is the only one of Sir Francis's buildings that does not appeal to me. Quite different in atmosphere is the church of St Lawrence behind the mausoleum. This was rebuilt in 1751–63 with the intention of attracting the young and lively, and it succeeded, triumphantly. It has a splendidly large, open, airy nave, with a ceiling following the design of the Temple of the Sun at Palmyra. The floors of both nave and chancel have marble paving with various patterns. To preserve the impression of uncluttered space, the pulpit was replaced by three carved armchairs, comfortable and beautiful to look at. On the chancel ceiling is a painting of the Last Supper, by Giovanni Borgnis, with the right eye of Judas painted to follow the viewer everywhere in the church. The church tower has the famous golden ball on top; this is 6 metres round, and can seat about eight people. One used to be able to enter the ball,

but this is no longer allowed due to past vandalism. However, a climb up the tower is still worth while for the view. One can see the mausoleum, and straight down the A40 to High Wycombe. More attractively, one can see West Wycombe Park, the house and the surrounding Chiltern Hills.

If you are returning to London at the end of this stage, there are buses to High Wycombe station, but these are somewhat infrequent on Sundays. One can walk to High Wycombe from the map by footpaths. Unfortunately, a new housing estate has been built obstructing some footpaths, and leaving rubbish and mess on the paths that are left. A clean-up campaign is called for, so that the countryside can match the tidy new houses. For those staying overnight at Bradenham Youth Hostel, a walk along the ridge from West Wycombe church is exhilarating, and is much better than the long road walk. The hostel is a simple self-catering one; it is rather cold in winter, but has the spirit of a 'true' hostel. While there, you can idle on the extensive village green. As with West Wycombe, the village is owned by the National Trust, and has some old and picturesque cottages. At the top of the green is the church and adjoining it, the manor house. This is famous as the place where Disraeli grew up, and is described in his book *Endymion*.

Route

From Marlow station, along Station Road, down Pound Lane opposite, and then, opposite car park, turn right along alley to road. Here turn right for 20 metres then turn left into Oxford Road for the start of the route. Follow this road until left bend, then right into Chiltern Road. In 70 metres left up enclosed path with allotments on right (good views back over Marlow). Follow path to entrance of Blounts Farm where right along righthand track to Woodside Farm. Bear right at track junction at trees. Keep on lower track and then descend left with fence and open field on right to lane. Cross and up steep enclosed bridle path to corner by End Farm. Left along road which soon becomes a track. At garden go right of beech

West Wycombe House

hedge and continue uphill on long, enclosed path to reach Copy Farm.

Turn right along road for 400 metres, then opposite cottage at Copy Green, bear left along a wide track and descend to Shillingridge Wood. Here take righthand path and follow wide track in wood which later climbs uphill. After passing an iron gate on left take left fork to stile. Over stile and right along top of fields. Across open space between fields to stile leading to enclosed path with pines on left.

At bridle path turn left for 30 metres to Bluey's Farm. Here turn right along bridle path to cross stile by gate. At end of field, through small gate on left, inset into wood. Now ahead along bridle path, ignoring all turns for 1 mile. At wood end keep right at fork on track, with field on right, to road. Left along B482 for 300 metres, then right across stile to cross field to wood.

Ahead through wood following track uphill (30°), keeping left at fork to reach waterworks. Path joins track descending from waterworks. After 150 metres, right along path, opposite manhole cover in field on left. Path is indistinct at first but soon becoming clearer as it enters the wood. At end right into road and cross bridge over M40 (818920).

At far end of bridge turn left along farm road to Pyatt's Farm. Beyond farm, the road becomes a track. Ahead along this, up and down hill, until it passes under a line of pylons. Now pass a small farm on right and a house on left, soon to reach a lane. Left and after 800 metres right along A40. Cross, with toilets and shop on right, and ascend hill to Mausoleum (827949). (For Bradenham Youth Hostel, continue along ridge for a mile, then down right under railway to Bradenham.)

Descend from far side of Mausoleum down grassy hill (130°) towards A40 and High Wycombe. At bottom of hill right along lane for a few metres then left over stile with a footpath sign. After 150 metres, right through gate and fence on to road, with Flint Hall Farm on left.

Cross A4010 to continue on route. To get to High Wycombe station, right 250 metres to junction A40 and A4010. Catch a bus from here to High Wycombe Station, or longer via difficult paths on left-hand hill.

Information

Distance	8 miles; total 56½ miles. Map 175.
Stations	Marlow: hourly from Maidenhead, no Sunday service. High Wycombe: hourly to Marylebone. Saunderton: rush hours only, not on Sundays.
Buses	High Wycombe: to Great Missenden, Alder 27 hourly, two-hourly Sundays; to West Wycombe, Alder 39, 40 and 41 irregular half-hourly and hourly on Sundays; to Windsor, London Country 441 hourly.
Admission	West Wycombe house and grounds, June, Monday–Friday, 2.15–6 p.m. July and August, every day except Saturdays, 2.15–6 p.m. Garden only, open same hours, plus Easter and Spring bank holidays. West Wycombe church, free: charge made for tower. West Wycombe caves, March–May and late September 1–6 p.m. May–August 11 a.m.–6 p.m. October–February weekends 12–4 p.m.
Refreshments	Royal Oak at Bovingdon Green (835870). West Wycombe: café, restaurant, George and Dragon, Plough Inn and sometimes teas at village hall.
Accommodation	Bradenham Youth Hostel, High Wycombe, Princes Risborough, West Wycombe.

This stage of the walk is through the heart of the Chilterns, and goes uphill and down to valley again four times in the 8 miles. It is a short section and there are no major 'sights' on the route, but you will find the miles take a long while to cover. The hills are tiring, and the scenery makes you want to linger. This is certainly true on the tops of the hills, when you can pause to regain breath, and admire the woods and the steep-sided valleys, where the roads run.

The Chilterns have their main ridge furthest from London, running NE to SW, and with a steep drop on its northern side. This main ridge is a splendid walk, and has the modern Ridgeway long distance footpath running along it, following the general line of the prehistoric path from Ivinghoe to Avebury. Our walk is equally good—but different—going about 4 miles SE of this and so crossing the subsidiary ridges running up to the main ridge from the SE. This gives us all the ups and downs as we cross these ridges and the valleys between. The Chilterns are chalk hills and the moisture sinks through the ground, making the valleys dry ones until we get to the Misbourne at Great Missenden. Fortunately, in the villages on the way there are a number of pubs where we can slake our thirst.

The walk starts from West Wycombe, but the nearest station is at High Wycombe. This is famous for furniture-making and several household names have factories here. The industry started with the making of Windsor chairs from the beechwoods around High Wycombe. The people who made the chairs were called 'bodgers' and this name persists in the area. Elsewhere the word has degenerated, and is used about someone who does a rough, crude job of making something—rather unfair to the original chairmakers! The factories are pleasant enough, but the houses spreading up the hills make the immediate area unattractive. The centre of High Wycombe is an abomination, particularly around the bus station, where the quantity of roads seems deliberately designed to be as ugly, inconvenient and dangerous to pedestrians as could be. High Wycombe has an attractive

name, but I was very disappointed when I first saw it. If you
have time to spare, however, the church on the north side of
the High Street is of thirteenth-century foundation and has a
60-metre nave. There is also the Guild Hall (1757) and Little
Market House (1761).

About a mile from the centre, but off our route, is
Hughenden Manor, once the home of Disraeli, now owned by
the National Trust and open to the public. The house was
bought by Disraeli in 1847, and he lived there until his death.
It has many of his possessions, books and pictures, and
preserves the Victorian atmosphere of his day. It is
surrounded by good parkland in which to sit or wander.

Back on the route, the path leaves West Wycombe to go up
a long hill which gives excellent views, looking backwards, of
the church and the golden ball. The way then goes through
the heavily wooded Naphill Common, where it is easy to get
lost among a multiplicity of paths—there is a conflict between
going through the best part of the wood furthest from the
houses, or sticking close to them to be sure of the way. The
route comes out at Naphill village. Up the road is a large Air
Force base, and, probably because of this, there is a bus
service from Naphill to High Wycombe. The route goes past
the Black Lion pub, which is small and hospitable, set
amongst the trees with a little green outside; but it can be very
crowded on Saturday nights.

After this the switchbacking starts, going down to North
Dean, and up and down to Bryants Bottom, up again, down
to another valley, and then a last up to the edge of Prestwood.
This is a large village with shops and pubs, and is on the bus
route between High Wycombe and Great Missenden. 1½ miles
NE from here is Hampden House, once the home of John
Hampden (1595–1643). John Hampden fought a long battle in
the courts against a levy of twenty shillings on him for 'ship
money'. This was a tax Charles I sought to impose without
the authority of parliament, and Hampden fought the case as
a matter of principle. As opponents pointed out, he could well
afford to pay! Hampden lost the case, as so many good causes
do lose in the courts, and Charles tried to have him arrested in

View back to West Wycombe

Parliament—just one of the sparks that brought about the Civil War. Hampden escaped from the attempted arrest, but was killed by Prince Rupert in the early stages of the war. It might be worthwhile going a little out of our way to pay homage to Hampden's memory. (There are no hills on the way!)

A couple of miles after Prestwood, we come to the edge of Great Missenden, by the Black Horse, a small pub which provides good home-made pasties. The meadow by this is called the Mobwell, where in wet weather there is a small stream. This is the start of the Misbourne, which flows through Great Missenden, Amersham and Chalfont, to join the Colne at Uxbridge. The name 'bourne' means a seasonal stream, normally in the chalk area, which in drier times goes underground. 1976 showed the suffix to be very appropriate for the Misbourne.

Great Missenden is a small country town, not too built up

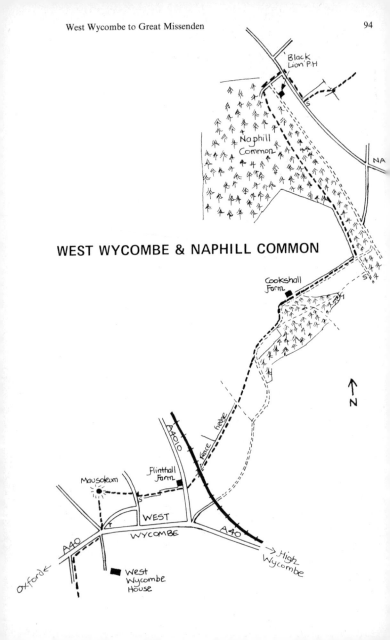

Black Lion P.H

Naphill Common

NA

WEST WYCOMBE & NAPHILL COMMON

Cookshall Farm

S

N →

A4010

lane verge

Mausoleum

Flinthall Farm

S

WEST WYCOMBE

A40

Oxford ←

A40

→ High Wycombe

West Wycombe House

or spectacular and with a pleasant atmosphere. It has a good supply of shops, and one café, the Corner Café, which will do breakfasts. Its two historical places, the church and the abbey, are both rather disappointing. The church has existed for centuries, but was heavily restored and added to in 1900. There are some interesting brasses and memorials inside the church. Great Missenden Abbey, nearby, was founded in 1133 for Augustinian canons, and was visited several times by Henry III.

It was dissolved in 1538 and thereafter occupied by different families. Since 1947, it has been a residential adult college. It looks a Regency Gothic mansion on the outside, but parts of the medieval monastic structure do survive. The sixteenth-century Red Lion in the High Street serves Youngs' and Ruddles' ales, and both hot and cold snacks with omelettes and ploughman's lunches.

There are good train services from Great Missenden, but if you wish to stay overnight, Lee Gate Youth Hostel is convenient: a mile off the route, a little way along the next stage.

Route

From High Wycombe station take a bus to West Wycombe (or walk 2½ miles) to junction A40 and A4010. Right on A4010 for 250 metres till opposite Flint Hall Farm and start of route. Here right and take path diagonally across field to gate under railway bridge. Under bridge and ahead uphill with wire fence on left. Path later descends to cross tracks. Over stile and continue uphill across field with good views back to the Mausoleum. Cross stile and soon join lane to Cookshall Farm.

The obvious and easiest route here is to continue along this lane, keeping to the right of the farm until 500 metres after farm, and come to a cross track just in the woods at Naphill Common. However, the 'correct' public footpath route leaves the lane just before the farm, goes right, through a gate, into a wood and on path for 200 metres. At cross paths, go left slightly uphill on path for length of wood till emerge at gate. Cross field to stile at other side, to another wood where keep left just inside this till meet lane and other route (847963).

Take first left-hand track, just inside wood, and continue in this direction (340°). When field on left starts bearing left, take second left path and keep on for 500 metres till meet gravel track, where bear right to road (841976).

Naphill Common is a heavily wooded place. Keep more to right than left if you haven't a compass, so that you keep houses on the right in sight.

At road, right, pass Black Lion, and after 200 metres left over stile and cross to far right-hand corner of field to stile. Slightly left, to go straight across wide field to hedge where cross stile, left over iron fence and diagonally across field to woods. Over stile into woods, later, when descending, take right fork down to stile and into field, where go to left corner. Cross stile and turn right on road to T-junction (850985). Here left for 70 metres, then right at path sign, over stile and uphill at edge of field. Continue left over stile into wood, then immediately right uphill and ahead past shack to join lane, where left along tarmac drive.

Tarmac ceases, but ahead, past sign to little Piggots. Keep wood on right and almost at end, facing end house, turn right into wood. Take left fork and go downhill. Cross stile by electricity pole and down to road at stile. Left, and then right opposite bus stop, along narrow enclosed path. Ahead up steep hill under electricity wires parallel to path, through Dennerhill Farm to T-junction. Turn right and after 50 metres left into lane. Along lane and left at farm to stile at left of gate. Cross and continue downhill passing under high voltage cables with hedge on right. At end, cross road to stile on other side. Ahead uphill to wood. Cross stile, and path goes into wood bearing slightly left. Keep ahead through wood to its end by stile, then ahead with hedge on right through two fields, over a stile, then ahead to a stile on far side of third field to a road at outskirts of Prestwood. Right along road soon to reach a cross roads. Ahead into Greenlands Lane and almost immediately right into Kiln Road.

Just after this road bends left, go right, in front of row of yellow cottages to reach Laurel Close (don't go right here) and ahead for 200 metres, then left at T-junction by path sign into a tarmac road (don't turn sharp left into an unmade road). Ahead, passing footpath signs to left and right, to a T-junction where right into Moat Lane. Ahead for 200 metres to footpath sign on left.

Left at sign (Prestwood Farm) along concrete track. Over stile and follow black and white posts and along right edge of grass field. Enter wood and follow white arrows along path slightly downhill, over stile and then along the left edge of field, left of house and along drive to road. Turn right and after 100 metres left along track (Coney Hill). After 100 metres turn right just before bungalow along track. When track ends, ahead with hedge on right to reach right-hand corner of field. Don't leave field yet, but continue on for another 70 metres, still with hedge on right, to next corner, where cross stile. Go half-right to pass under railway. Ahead across field to stile at road, where right and pass Black Horse. Immediately beyond this, left over stile and then right across field with football pitch, to stile/gate 30 metres from right-hand corner of field. In next field, aim for far left corner of field, and to left of radio mast, to reach A413 at stile and footpath sign. (To end at Great Missenden, right on road for 300 metres, then right again to reach Great Missenden station in 500 metres.) If continuing on route it is easiest to cross road by a cattle tunnel 30 metres on past stile.

Information

Distance	8 miles; total 64½. Map 165.
Stations	High Wycombe: hourly to Marylebone. Great Missenden: hourly to Marylebone.
Buses	High Wycombe to West Wycombe, frequently weekdays, about one an hour Sundays, Alder 39, 40, 41. High Wycombe to Great Missenden via Prestwood, hourly, two-hourly Sundays, Alder 27.

Admission	Hughenden Manor, February–November, Wednesday, Thursday, Friday, 2–6 p.m. Saturday and Sunday 12.30–6 p.m., or sunset if earlier.
Refreshments	Black Lion at Naphill, pubs at Prestwood, Black Horse outside Great Missenden, Red Lion and Corner Café at Great Missenden.
Accommodation	Difficult. Lee Gate Youth Hostel, Amersham, High Wycombe.

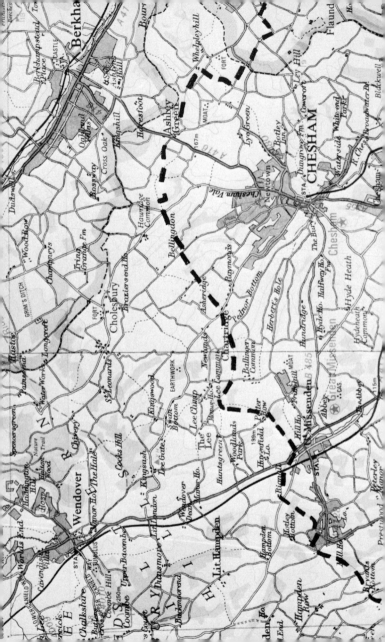

This section is another short one, with no buildings or places of particular note—it is just a jolly good walk. You may wish to combine this stage with the next, particularly if you stayed at Lee Gate Youth Hostel, and make Ashley Green a lunchtime stop. (There is a good pub there, if you do!) Against this, the stage is hilly with five climbs up from valleys. The route does a circuit of Chesham, and the ridges radiate from there like the fingers of a hand. The little roads are on the tops of the ridges and you cross from one to the next across the dry chalk valleys.

These are beautiful, remote little valleys, ideal for picnicking, dreaming and lazing before having to make the steep climb out to the next ridge. The views are of grass fields with sheep, and of woods scattered along the hillsides, a pastoral landscape which seems far indeed from London. The villages and hamlets spread along the ridge tops are small and nothing special, but they have a peaceful air. If you are doing the stage by itself, there are two good pubs half-way along.

The stage starts from Great Missenden, and if you come by train, you travel along the Misbourne valley from Amersham and pass Little Missenden, where the ex-Prime Minister, Harold Wilson, has a country house. The route begins with a good climb up and then by strips of woods to a narrow road by the edge of Ballinger. We are about $1\frac{1}{2}$ miles from Lee Gate Youth Hostel—a simple self-catering one. Near the Lee, at a bend in the road, is a large figurehead, which comes from the *Howe* of the 1860s. The figure—the torso of Earl Howe— can be a disturbing sight at night.

The path from Ballinger starts by the edge of a wood at the side of Ballinger Bottom, and runs by the edge of other small woods to Chartridge. It makes a satisfying section of the route, particularly in autumn, with a good tramp through the beech leaves. There is a pub in Chartridge, and, after a descent to the next valley, a climb up brings one to a second pub, the Blue Ball, rather posh but welcoming, and providing food.

The route to the end at Ashley Green is a little complicated

with one or two diversions, new paddocks and unofficial short
(or long!) cuts, so follow the directions with care, and
interpret them with discretion, if the field boundaries have
changed since my description! It is a lonely section with good
views, so it is worth the effort. After the Blue Ball, there is a
drop through a wood to a long bottom with steep hills on
either side. We are less than a mile from the edge of Chesham,
but it seems more like the Welsh border!

There is a stiff climb after this beautiful spot, and, in
contrast, a drop to the road by an untidy path to old car
sumps at a garage! There is then a last gentler hill, with bigger
fields and an area with many alterations from the map, to
reach Ashley Green. This has a welcoming pub, the Eagle, a
shop, post office, and bus service. The bus is an hourly service
(two-hourly on Sundays) to the station at Berkhamsted,
although there are some good paths if you prefer to finish in

Path to Blue Ball, nr Amersham

BALLINGER - CHARTRIDGE

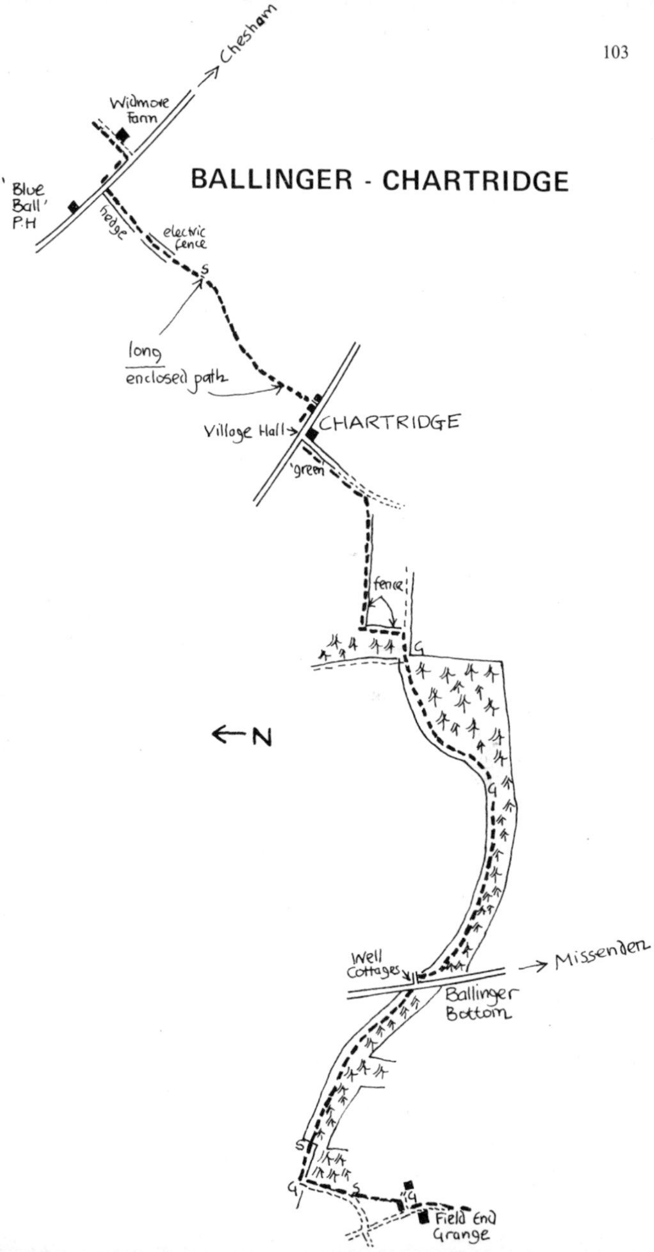

→ Chesham

Widmore Farm

'Blue Ball' P.H

hedge

electric fence

S

long enclosed path

Village Hall → CHARTRIDGE

'green'

fence

G

← N

Well Cottages

→ Missenden

Ballinger Bottom

S

G

S

G

Field End Grange

style. In the other direction, the bus goes to Chesham, and
even on to Windsor, if you wish to return on your tracks for a
car left behind.

Route

From Great Missenden station right along the A4128 to the
A413. Left along this for 300 metres, cross road by large
traffic sign, and right to go ahead along a wide track, under
pylons. Later keep to left of hedge to reach kissing-gate in top
right-hand corner of field. Continue along an enclosed path to
join a drive later. At end of drive, left along road for 300
metres to reach a white house on right. Here go right by
footpath sign, cross stile and then half turn left across field.
Over two stiles and ahead across next two fields passing under
power lines. In far corner of the second field, over stile ahead
(not the one on left), and left to follow hedge to field corner,
where keep right with hedge still on left. Ahead to join a track
which passes Field End Grange on left. Just beyond, turn
right along track, through gate and then go left across a field
descending to a stile. Turn right along a bridle path soon to
reach a stile and gate, where turn right. Follow with wood on
right for 50 metres, cross stile and enter wood. Continue
through wood until path emerges at road by Ballinger
Bottom.

   Cross road and enter lane opposite marked 'Well Cottages'.
After 50 metres right at footpath sign, and follow path at left
edge of wood all the way until wood ends at a gate. Go
through gate and along an enclosed path which ends at a gate
into a wood. Turn left in wood, then right at bottom of hill
and continue until wood ends on right. Keep ahead, passing
gate on right. A wood is now on your left. At 100 metres left
and proceed uphill on path with wire fence on right. At field
corner, right along track with wire fence still on right. At end
left along farm track, which leads to T-junction with
Chartridge Village Hall on right.

   Turn right on road and, after 150 metres, left at footpath
sign between houses, with Baptist church on right. Ahead
along a track which soon becomes a long enclosed path.

Garage and path nr Ashley Green

Over stile, keep to right edge of field and then ahead uphill
between electric fences, then ahead with hedge on left to reach
road. The Blue Ball is 100 metres on left. Right along road for
100 metres, then left up track by Widmore Farm.

Ahead on track soon to enter wood. Along obvious middle
stony path. Bear right at bottom of hill into neck of wood,
and after 150 metres left out of wood over stile. Ahead up hill
and along right of hedge to Bellingdon. Turn right along
road, and after 100 metres left along an enclosed path. After
250 metres, turn right at a cottage. 100 metres further on, left
into field with hedge on left. Keep to edge of field and cross
stile to intersect with horse-ride in wood. (The official right of
way now goes right 300 metres along edge of wood, then left
through wood downhill, and left again at bottom of field for
400 metres, but locals use the following short cut to field at
X.)

Cross this horse-ride and ahead across field to left, and go

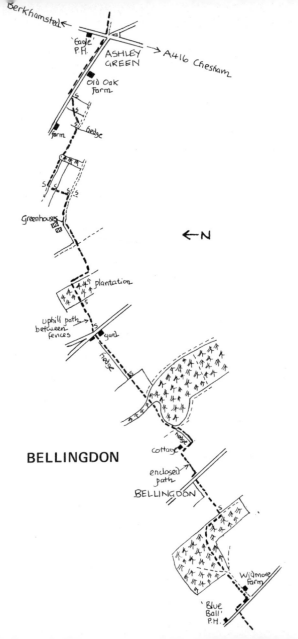

Berkhamsted ←

'Eagle' P.H.

ASHLEY GREEN

→ A416 Chesham

Old Oak Farm

S
S
S hedge
farm

←N

Greenhouses

plantation

uphill path between fences
S gate
hedge
S

BELLINGDON

cottage

enclosed path

BELLINGDON

S

Widmore Farm

'Blue Ball' P.H.

downhill keeping wood on right all the way to the bottom. At valley bottom find way through narrow strip of woodland and over stile or fence into field (X). Climb up slope to stile in hedge 50 metres from right hand corner of field. Over stile, through gap in right hedge, then ahead by right of hedgerow over broad ridge. Descend by several stiles, through paddock to road by a scruffy yard (957055).

Cross road and up path opposite, between barbed wire fences, through a small plantation and enter a field. Here the path has been diverted and marked with small signs. Turn right, as signposted. After about 100 metres, sharp left along clear track across field. At end of field, go straight over cross path and continue ahead on farm track. This bends right and about 150 metres later, a footpath crosses track at right angles via two stiles. Take left-hand path, passing two oak trees, crossing a fence and making for a stile in hedge.

Cross stile and turn right along path between hedges to enter small coppice. When path bears right, turn left to leave wood and then right to cross field (no longer an orchard as on map). Keep farm buildings on left to soon join farm track. Pass through gap in trees and then climb stile on left to enter a paddock. Make for stile on right half way down side of the paddock. Ahead to road where right to Ashley Green (977052). Eagle pub and shop 50 metres on left.

(To end walk, catch a bus here to Berkhamsted or Chesham, or go left on road to Berkhamsted in two miles).

Information

Distance	7 miles; total $71\frac{1}{2}$ miles. Map 165.
Stations	Great Missenden: hourly to Marylebone. Berkhamsted: half-hourly, hourly on Sundays, to Euston. Amersham: half-hourly to Baker Street, and Marylebone on weekdays.

Buses   Berkhamsted to Amersham (and Windsor)
via Ashley Green: London Country 353,
hourly, two-hourly on Sundays.
Chartridge and Ballinger to Chesham:
London Country 348, about two-hourly.
No Sunday service.

Refreshments   Chartridge (933037), Eagle at Ashley
Green.
Blue Ball (938046) is now closed.

Accommodation   Amersham, Berkhamsted, Hemel Hempstead.

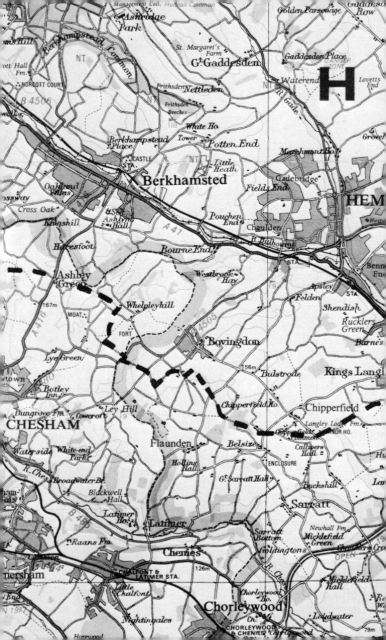

This stage is the last stretch of our long walk through the Chilterns. This time, instead of crossing from ridge to ridge, we are on the broad upland between the Chess Valley in the south and the Bulborne valley in the north. It makes a good breezy walk, with wider and different views. There are more ploughed fields than sheep pastures to see, and some of the paths can be decidedly muddy.

The easiest way to get to the start at Ashley Green is from Berkhamsted station. Easily missed are the remains of the eleventh-century Berkhamsted Castle just behind the station. It is one of the earliest Norman castles, though only the earthworks, moat and some thirteenth-century siege works remain. It was a favourite royal residence up till the time of Queen Elizabeth. Chaucer, Thomas à Becket and Henry VIII all visited here. There is a good footpath at the start to Ashley Green, two miles away, or you could catch a bus, rather infrequent on Sundays.

The Countryway route starts with a drop to a valley and a steep climb afterwards—reminiscent of the last stage, except that this is the only one this time! Soon after this, there are some wide bridleways near Moors Farm, which can be very sticky and unpleasant to walk in winter. They mark the end of Buckinghamshire and we enter Hertfordshire by a narrow track in a long thin wood, leading to Pudds Cross. Just past here, the route makes a dog-leg past some disused army huts to get to Bovingdon Green—there is a footpath shortcut on the map, but sand quarrying has made this so difficult to follow that this alternative has been taken. Bovingdon Green is a peaceful place, with a large village green and a convenient pub for sandwiches. Then it is on by lanes and woods to Chipperfield Common.

The common is a fascinating place, and except near the village, is heavily wooded with some splendid beeches and limes. Although it is narrow and has houses right on its edge, it has so many paths it is quite easy to get lost. The southernmost path, near the houses, can get churned up by horses, so it is best to avoid this, though all the paths seem to

lead back to it, or to the village on the other side. There is a pub here with some comfortable grass nearby to sit on, and on Tower Hill is the Boot. This is a well-kept old pub which provides soup and pâté.

Also on Chipperfield Common is a small pool, called the Apostles Pool, because of the twelve large lime trees around it. From just past this pool there is a good striding path leading to the end of the stage at Kings Langley. This is a small town, half-way between Watford and Berkhamsted, with a fifteenth-century church and a collection of shops. Despite its present-day appearance, it is famous in history.

Edward II and Edward III lived here, and Edward, Duke of York, and Richard II are buried here. The Grand Union canal, that forerunner of the railway and the M1, runs through Kings Langley. This section was part of the Grand Junction Canal, built around 1800 to link the Midlands canals at Braunston with the Thames at Brentford. It was constructed with a wide channel to encourage commercial traffic, but its links to other canals were kept so narrow that only the standard 2-metre craft were able to use it. Thus the only real attempt to give Britain proper commercial waterways failed. The stretch on our route is rather sad and not scenic, but a pleasant time can be had watching the pleasure craft going through the lock. About 400 metres from the railway station is a small, cheap but good, café where you can finish the day with egg on toast and a good cup of tea. Unfortunately it is not open on Saturday afternoons or Sundays—one reason for doing this stage on a weekday!

Route

From Berkhamsted station walk the 2 miles to Ashley Green or catch the London Country 353 bus.

At Ashley Green cross roads, bear left of junction across green to enter track by footpath sign, soon giving on to small field. Keep fences on left, then hedge, until track divides at end of line of trees. Take right-hand track between fences uphill and left. Keep on same track across field for 100 metres

Sweet Chestnut on Chipperfield Common

(130°) to stile, then across next field to pylon and stile at bottom of valley.

Cross stile and bear half-left (100°) and climb hill to pass to right of a line of trees, and then to stile 100 metres in from right edge of thin line of woodland—you may be able to follow a faint track—to come out at a bend on a wide farm track between trees. Take right fork of track uphill and continue to farm with a tennis court on left. Ahead (140°), over stile and cross fields by faint path for 500 metres with no hedges until a farm track crosses at right angles. Take right track and reach road after 100 metres. Cross road and follow bridle path opposite into wood. On leaving wood go left on track, which can be very muddy in winter. This goes round field edge to Moors Farm, where past barns turn left on another farm track. This later has a hedge on left and comes to the B4505 road (996032).

Right on main road for 100 metres and left on path at car park by bridlepath, going through wood between lines of trees and then past a house, Green Acres, to road at Pudds Cross. Follow road opposite, Shantock Hall Lane, for 400 metres, then left on path just before a house, Beechcroft. Continue by left side of woodland and at end of wood, ahead on wide path with laurel hedge on left to road and bridlepath sign at Bovingdon Green. Turn right on to Green and keeping on right of it aim for road on far side of Green, just before road junction and pub. Cross road to path marked Bovingdon.

Continue for 50 metres with hedge on right until a stile, then with hedge on left. Turn right before stile and continue by wire fence to right-hand opposite side of field.

Continue in new direction (160°), at first between fences, until road is reached at junction (020022).

Cross road and go up lane opposite until after 900 metres lane bends suddenly to the right inside wood. Here take footpath ahead and continue through, taking left fork. Cross over track with farm on left and continuing with hedge on left drop down to road in the valley. Turn left at road and immediately right up road to Chipperfield. The common soon

Grand Union Canal, Kings Langley
Apostles Pool, Chipperfield

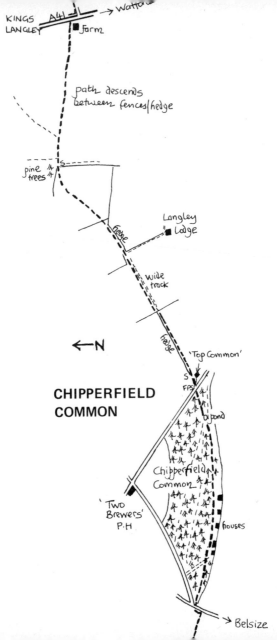

KINGS LANGLEY — A41 → Watford

farm

116

path descends between fences/hedge

pine trees

Langley Lodge

hedge

wide track

hedge

← N

'Top Common'

S FPS

Di pond

CHIPPERFIELD COMMON

Chipperfield Common

'Two Brewers' P.H

houses

→ Belsize

appears on the right. Make for opposite end (east) of common, following your nose through the middle (110°), avoiding the southernmost path which is a muddy horse-ride. If you catch occasional glimpses of houses on the right you are correct. Later you should pass a small pond on the right—this is the Apostles Pool, so called because of the twelve trees round it.

From the seat on the north side of the pond go left between third and fourth tree and after 70 metres, reach road opposite house—Top Common (049012).

Cross road and take path signposted to Kings Langley (1¾ miles). After 60 metres, go left and then ahead, cross two stiles and follow path with hedge on left. After joining a wide farm track take stile on left and keep hedge on right. Cross a new stile and follow by hedge to corner of field where turn left and then immediately right over a stile between electric fences. Cross field diagonally towards fir trees. Climb stile and follow path between fences (ignoring turnings on left), and later between hedge and fence down to farm and A41 road. Right for 100 metres then left down lane at derestriction signs. Follow lane over canal and up to road at Kings Langley station. Left along road to continue. Very good, cheap café 400 metres on left along road.

Information

Distance	8½ miles, total 80 miles. Maps 165 and 166.
Stations	Berkhamsted: half-hourly, hourly on Sundays, to Euston. Kings Langley: hourly to Euston.
Buses	Berkhamsted to Ashley Green: London Country 353 hourly, two-hourly Sundays.
Admission	Berkhamsted Castle. Standard Department of the Environment hours.

Refreshments   Bovingdon (013028), the Boot at
Chipperfield. Small, good café just past
Kings Langley station. 8.00 a.m.–4.30 p.m.
weekdays and 1 p.m. Saturdays. Closed
Sundays.

Accommodation   Kings Langley, Hemel Hempstead.

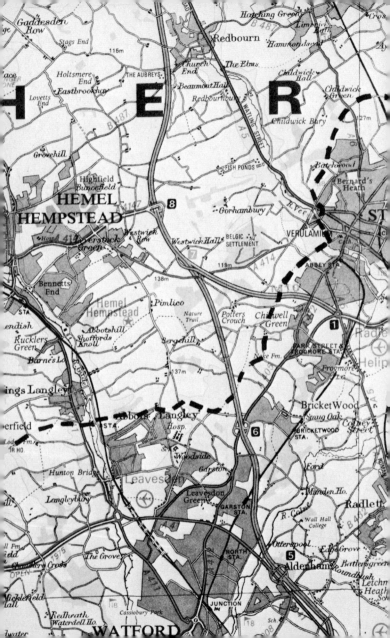

This section is a short one, but there is so much to see in St Albans that one day may not be enough. Rose enthusiasts may find it difficult even to reach there as the Rose Society's gardens are on the way. The route as a whole skirts the edge of the built-up area stretching from Watford to St Albans, and crosses two motorways. Not surprisingly, the paths have a certain urban look, but many are still rural.

The route starts by going past the Ovaltine egg farm, which is no longer open to the public but you can still compare the outside with advertisements. Nearby is Bedmond, the birthplace of Nicholas Breakspear, who, as Adrian IV, was the only Englishman to become Pope. He reigned from 1154 to 1159 and is said to have granted Henry II permission to conquer Ireland.

The path keeps close to the town until after going under the M1, when it becomes more rural till it leads up to Bone Hill by the side of the National Rose Society's gardens. These contain twelve acres of display gardens and trial grounds, and are open to the public during the summer. There are fifteen hundred varieties of roses on display, including those on trial, so there is ample opportunity to pick one's favourite. There are old-fashioned garden roses, wild roses, miniature roses, and the more usual types. The layman will find plenty to delight him or her with the massed beds of colour and the many fragrant scents. The gardens are at the top of a hill, and in stormy weather the amateur like myself wonders how such splendid flowers can be grown. Books, prints and other mementoes can be obtained and there is also a cafeteria. For other refreshments, at Chiswell Green not far away is the Three Hammers, which does good pub lunches on weekdays.

On the route itself, we cut down a hill through a new housing estate to the south-eastern corner of Verulamium Park. This is a large park, with several sports pitches, tea rooms and so on, but it is also the southern half of the old Roman city of Verulamium. This was one of the first towns built by the Romans after the invasion of AD 43, and was situated where a community of the Catuvellauni had their

homes, near to their stronghold at Prae Wood. Boadicea, in
the uprising she led in AD 60–61, completely destroyed the
town, and building did not start again for ten to fifteen years.
Then, over the years, a town covering two hundred acres was
built up, with blocks of shops, centrally heated houses,
basilica, forum, piped water, temple and theatre. The whole
was enclosed by fortifications, the last and largest of which
was the third-century town wall.

This wall was 2 miles long, 6 metres high and about 3
metres thick at the base, narrowing to about 2 metres at the
top, with towers at intervals along it. Outside it was a flat
area—the berm—6 metres wide, then a ditch, 25 metres wide.
Altogether, some pretty formidable defences!

Our route goes from the entrance to the park along the
causeway formed by the berm, with the ditch on our right and
the wall, at its most impressive, on our left. There are new
trees growing in the ditch and behind the wall, making the
causeway into a shaded avenue. We soon come to the lake
and can go either side of it to leave the park and come on to
St Michael's Street. Up here on the left is the Verulamium
Museum, which contains a large number of finds from the
Roman town. There are some good mosaics from the larger
houses, particularly a shell-motif pavement and the lion
mosaic. There is also a large topographical model of the town
as it might have appeared in the third century, showing the
great extent of the town. It is well worth visiting even if you
can't avoid the hordes of children on school visits!

Further along, across the main A414 (pedestrian crossing),
are the remains of the Roman theatre, unique in Britain. It
looks most impressive, though you should discount the large
horseshoe shaped earth mound which has been made from the
excavations. You can see the stage, the dressing rooms, and
the area where the audience used to sit on wooden benches.
Next to the theatre are the remains of shops from different
eras of the town.

The last notable Roman remains are those of the hypocaust
or private bath wing, in a large house, in the middle of the
park. There is a large pavement mosaic under which was the

Rose Garden, Bone Hill

tepidarium or warm room. Bathers started here before moving to one of the hot rooms on either side. Outside the house wall is the floor of the fire-pit from which flues led warm air to the bathing-rooms.

The Countryway carries on from St Michael's Street, away from the centre of St Albans. But St Albans has so much to offer, with the atmosphere of its old streets, inns and houses, and also the cathedral, that you should stay to see more of it. If you are leaving from the railway station you will need to go through the town centre anyway. There is a large variety of places to stay in St Albans, from cheap bed-and-breakfast to hotels, and a good tourist office to assist you. Have a lie-in too—most of the museums don't open till 10 a.m!

From the causeway in the park, the cathedral stands in front and dominates the view. Carry on up to it, passing Ye

Olde Fighting Cocks on the right. This is an old-looking inn and is in an attractive setting, but, perhaps because of its popularity, it lacks a 'local' feeling.

The Cathedral is thought to be on the site where England's first Christian martyr was executed in 209 in the reign of the Emperor Severus. Alban, a Briton but also a Roman citizen, sheltered a British priest on the run. He was converted by him, and when the priest was traced to Alban's home, Alban changed cloaks with the priest and was arrested in his place. Alban refused to recant and was executed. A monastic shrine was built here, and later, in 793, Offa, King of Mercia, founded an abbey and restarted the monastery.

The present building was begun by the Normans in 1077 and the tower and main transept walls still remain from then. The outer buildings were demolished with the dissolution of the monasteries, and the abbey was then bought by St Albans for a parish church. It was too big for the town to maintain and the church fell into disrepair. Restoration was started in the late nineteenth century, but was going very slowly until Lord Grimthorpe, a strong-willed millionaire, took the work over. He ignored the architects, had the work done his way and restored the church to its present glory.

Seen from outside, the cathedral looks astonishingly long and, at 170 metres, it is indeed the second largest in Britain. Entering by the west door you are immediately impressed by the large nave with its mixture of styles, Norman and later. At the eastern end can be seen various wall-paintings, dating back to 1215. The choir ceiling is decorated throughout with royal shields and monograms. The high altar screen was completed in 1489, but the statues were removed later and new ones made in the 1890s. At the eastern end of the church is the original reason for its existence, the Saint's Chapel with St Alban's shrine, where thousands of pilgrims came to see the bones of the saint. Finally, at the easternmost end of the church is the beautiful Lady Chapel, once a school. There is, of course, much else to see, with the old bells, carvings, brasses, and many stone scratchings to discover. There is an

Verulamium Park, St Albans (124–5)
St Albans Street

excellent little guide book, the Alban guide, to help you round the cathedral.

Now you have seen the main sights of St Albans, enjoy yourself wandering round the old streets and sampling some of the inns and shops. Fishpool Street and its continuations Romeland and George Street are attractive with a mixture of medieval and Georgian houses. French Row, so called because French soldiers were quartered here in 1216, has several buildings dating back to the fifteenth century. The Fleur-de-Lys Inn (1430) in the corner is where King John of France was kept prisoner. Opposite it is the old Clock Tower, built in 1410 and one of only two left in the country. It was the old curfew tower, and its bells used to summon townspeople to work at four a.m.!

In the Peasants' Revolt of 1380 the townspeople of St Albans extracted a charter of liberties from the Abbott and this was confirmed by the King. The local leader was William

Grindcobbe, and the people were encouraged by the famous rebel priest, John Ball, who used as his text, 'When Adam delved and Eve span, who was then a gentleman?' However, after Wat Tyler was killed and the rebels had put down their arms to go back to work, vengeance was exacted. All concessions that had been made were withdrawn and many rebel leaders executed. Both Grindcobbe and Ball were hanged, drawn and quartered at St Albans. Later, two battles were fought here during the Wars of the Roses. In one of them, in 1455, Henry VI was captured in a baker's shop.

Enough of this—let's enjoy our history in St Alban's old inns. However, there are so many you could get well under the weather if you tried them all in one day! They include the Bell (1452), King Harry (1505), White Lion (1594), and Old Kings Arms (1633). The Goat Inn, in Sopwell Lane, does good salads and is both ancient (fifteenth century) and welcoming. Take your pick, wander round and enjoy yourself.

Route

From Kings Langley station, right along road, and after 350 metres turn right under the railway. Bear right and follow main stony track uphill for 800 metres, past wood and cottage on right. At next track bend, through squeeze gate on right and diagonally across field (105°). At far side left through squeeze fence and along path, passing Ovaltine Dairy Farm. Keep on to road (096025).

Right, and after 120 metres left down Love Lane, signposted to Sergehill, 1½ miles. Ahead along track, through iron gate at end of recreation area, and along path. Over stile at end and along field following fence on left. Cross lane and left ahead across field (35°). At far side, right and follow hedge on left. Ahead to bridleway and on to road. 100 metres left along road, go left up track where footpath sign to Noke Lane, 1½ miles. Keep ahead to tunnel under M1 (117028).

Thirty metres out of tunnel, left at beech tree and follow path through wood. At field go left and follow track by line of trees to wide crossing track. Left for 10 metres, and then right on a wide track. On past Holt Farm to lane. Right for 180

Footpath from Bone Hill

metres, then left over stile hidden in hedge and with signpost to Chiswell Green. On through Noke Farm, past much farm machinery, and follow track (350°) going left, with wire fence on right, then on left in the next field (10°). Over a stile 50 metres on the right in hedge, and ahead (10°) to left side of tall hedge enclosing the National Rose Society gardens and on to lane at Bone Hill.

Right for 80 metres, then left opposite entrance (continue on for pub at Chiswell Green), and ahead for 200 metres across field (20°) to corner at lane bend. Ahead up lane, and at turn cross into wood and ahead up wide track to far side of wood. Right at end for 200 metres to stile at corner of wood, then left over footbridge.

Over M10 and ahead, going left round end of wood. After 50 metres, right down centre of field past large tree (45°). Left at edge of housing estate, for 50 metres, then right up a footpath between houses. Keep ahead across several minor

roads. Past a sports field on the right and on to main road. Cross and into Verulamium Park. Follow path, with Roman wall and park on left, to lake.

(Before lake, turn right down lane for Abbey station in 400 metres. For main line station, City station, ahead to the left of the cathedral, right on road, past clock tower and left at traffic lights, then first right down Victoria Street to reach station in 800 metres.) To continue the walk, left by far side of lake, right over a small bridge and left on path out of park, to emerge opposite Water Mill Museum. Cross road, right over bridge and fork left at Black Lion to go on Branch Road.

Information

Distance	7 miles; total 87 miles. Map 166.
Stations	Kings Langley: hourly to Euston. St Albans Abbey: forty-minute service, hourly on Sundays, to Watford. St Albans City: four an hour, two an hour on Sundays, to St Pancras.
Admission	National Rose Society, mid-June–September, Monday–Saturday, 9 a.m.–5 p.m., Sunday 2–6 p.m. Verulamium Museum (and hypocaust), March–October, weekdays 10 a.m.–5.30 p.m., Sundays 2–5.30 p.m November–February, weekdays 10 a.m.–4 p.m., Sundays 2–4 p.m. Roman theatre, April–October, Monday–Saturday, 10 a.m.–5.30 p.m., Sunday 2–5.30 p.m. November–March, close 4 p.m.
Refreshments	Café at Kings Langley. Three Hammers at Chiswell Green. Cafés, restaurants and many pubs in St Albans. The Goat in Sopwell Lane—good salads.
Accommodation	Good. Bed and breakfast and many hotels in St Albans.

St Albans to Brookmans Park 10½ miles

This stage goes through unspectacular but pleasant country round St Albans and skirting Hatfield; it stays rural practically the whole way, apart from the main roads it crosses. We stay at roughly the same level throughout (between 75 and 120 metres above sea level), so the little extra mileage on this section should not prove difficult. There are several interesting features, and a good supply of pubs on the way. The route starts by going through Batchwood golf course, a municipal course which looks quite attractive to me, a non-golfer. The club house at Batchwood Hall contains a restaurant open to all. We go past the edge of the parkland, across the A6, and by good paths to the village of Sandridge. This is a quiet place with some interesting old houses and a Norman church. The church was started in 1119; the nave walls, with octagonal piers, were built in 1160, and the font also dates from this period. The church has had many ups and downs over the centuries, some literally, and the end result is a rather pleasing little village church. Sandridge also has three pubs, with the Rose and Crown providing hot lunches on weekdays.

After Sandridge there is a good hollowed bridleway and then a section by Oak Farm, where the path has often been ploughed out and planted over, making it difficult to see the correct way. Follow the directions carefully. A little after this the path goes by the edge of Hatfield airfield, where Hawker-Siddeley used to test aircraft. The path was very overgrown here, but was cleared recently by local footpath workers. We come out at the Horseshoes on the A414, a good place for catching a bus to St Albans or Hatfield.

Hatfield House is about 2½ miles off the route, and is the home of the Cecil family. This large and impressive house was built in 1607–11, after James I had swapped his old palace and house here for the Cecils' previous house. In the grounds are the remains of the old Hatfield palace, including the banqueting room where Elizabeth I was kept virtually a prisoner during Mary's reign. Elizabeth was here, in Hatfield

Park, when she was brought the news of Mary's death and of her own accession to the throne. Back on the Countryway and about 1,200 metres from the A414, we come to the Plough, a pub buried away at the end of a narrow track. This started life in the seventeenth century as a remote alehouse serving the hamlet of Smallford, but is now an attractive old building. It serves good pub lunches, and becomes rather full later on.

The Plough is a useful stopping point before a short stretch of unattractive country, with the newly widened North London Orbital road and a quarrying area. Next comes Colney Heath, with a number of dull-looking pubs and a walk along a busy road until we have the relief of entering North Mymms Park. This is open parkland with a path across to St Mary's church at North Mymms. This was mostly built between 1330 and 1450 and is beautifully light and airy inside. There are some brasses in the church from between 1360 and 1590, long removed from their graves and now in the north wall of the chancel and by the priest's door.

There is also an altar tomb of Derbyshire alabaster, with an Elizabethan lady carved on the top, in a window recess in the north aisle. The west doorway is the best of the church fabric with its decorated shafting. In the porch of the church are ten or so boards listing the various charities set up to relieve local needs. There is reference in one to 'a field called Wants lying near to Muffets'. This refers to a farm once owned by Mr Thomas Muffet, whose daughter is thought to have been the original Little Miss Muffet.

It is possible to get a glimpse of North Mymms House across the park. This is a beautiful Elizabethan house built for Sir Ralph Coningsby in 1599. There are paintings inside by Bellini, Breughel, and Canaletto. Unfortunately, the house is not open to the public, although occasionally the grounds are.

After the peace of the park, we come to the A1 and the tiny hamlet of Water End. This is a good spot for refreshments, with a transport café and two pubs. The second one, the Old Maypole, is a well kept fifteenth-century inn with warming fires, old brasses, and reasonable food. It is too well carpeted

Batchwood Hall Golf Course, St Albans
Sandridge Village

for muddy boots, so leave them outside! The first pub, the Woodman, (Benskin Ales) has a path by the side signposted to Welham Green. This is not the original Countryway route, but it is worth going 400 metres along it to see the Swallowhole, where the Mimmshall brook disappears into a hole in the ground, in the middle of a rather marshy stretch of land. Water End is on the edge of the chalk and the stream goes into the chalk to make its way to the Lea Valley. The hole itself is about 1 metre across, but the last time I saw it, in 1976's dry summer, the stream had dried up before it reached the Swallowhole. Although the hole contained some water, it also contained rather a large collection of old tin cans.

A small diversion takes us back to the Countryway route at the bottom of a field with the ruins of a house at the far end. This was once Potterells Park. A little stream by the edge of this also vanishes, and again the water goes to the Lea. After this, we come out on the road by Welham Green, and 800 metres along the road brings us to Brookmans Park Hotel, a beautiful example of roadhouse gothic, and Brookmans Park station, for the journey home.

Route

The route starts from the Water Mill Museum at the corner of St Michael's Street and Fishpool Street. Follow the directions of the previous stage to get there through St Albans. Then, from the museum, right over bridge, fork left at Black Lion to go on Branch Road. At end, left and cross road, the A5. Right at roundabout and left after 50 metres to Batchwood Hall. After 300 metres right through iron gate, and follow right edge of golf course. When hedgerow stops, keep ahead to right of bunkers (40°) to pass between two posts in line of trees ahead. Keep ahead, in same direction, crossing a driveway and on old curved track, past footpath sign to leave course by iron gate.

Left and ahead to wood. Then right just inside or outside wood alongside Toulmin Drive. At end of wood, cross over grass to go diagonally left to far corner (360°). Over stile in hedge and follow fence on right. Through gate and ahead to

Interior of Sandridge Church

another stile by small wooden gate. Right and after 80 metres
left, join a track at wood edge and soon reach white gates and
A6. (146104).

Cross over and go up farm road opposite bridleway (to
Sandridge, $1\frac{1}{4}$ miles) to Cheapside Farm. Left at farm
buildings to an iron gate, where go right across field (110°) to
a gate and bridge over railway. Follow path ahead across
fields, keeping right of boundary, and keep ahead at all times
to reach lane. Cross, and across stiles, then across paddocks
to reach a recreation ground. Keep along left edge to road at
Sandridge, where there are toilets and shops. Left along road,
then right into House Lane, passing Rose and Crown on the
right.

Follow road out of village, and 300 metres past
derestriction signs, left on bridleway between hedgerows
(176099). Keep on the path till cross a lane, between wire
fences and then with wire fence on right. Where this ends,
straight on to wooden gate just before second farm (Oak
Farm), and here half left (110°) across field. The paths may be
a little hard to follow by this farm. But keep on, over stile to
far side and across next field (110°) to stile and road by a
bridleway sign. Across and along track to Beech Farm
(theoretically right 100 metres and left through woods to this
track), where right after first building, a concrete barn, and
follow main track to the end, ignoring gates leading off. After
800 metres reach edge of Aerodrome (197083) at 'Warning to
Trespassers' sign. Right over stile, follow hedge on left, over
stile at 250 metres. Here left inside wire fence and later with
airfield fence on left and then on narrow enclosed path to
emerge at Notcutts Nursery and road (A414) opposite the
Three Horseshoes (197078).

Cross road and follow path, later going past houses to lane,
where right, then at T-junction left over a hump-backed
bridge. 100 metres on, left along tarmac footpath across field.
On past the Plough (202069) and right on a lane. After old
barn left along footpath. Half-left across dual carriageway to
signed footpath. Keep to left of fence, then ahead on path
between fences, through gravel workings, then in same
direction across fields to reach the road at Colney Heath by

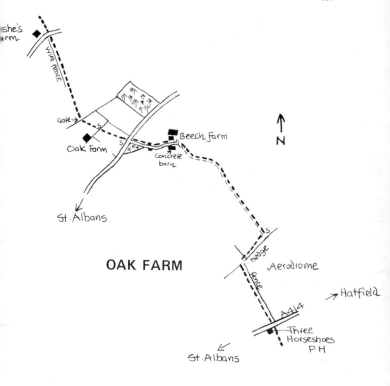

the Chalkdrawers. Right down road to cross roads, and left, with two pubs on right. Follow Tollgate Road (B6426) for 1,000 metres, then right at path signed to Water End, through wooden gate into parkland (218049).

Diagonally left across field, past fence corner (150°) to stile and narrow wooden bridge. Continue in roughly the same direction (140°), cross drive by stiles, and ahead into churchyard by right of church and along drive past cottages. After 50 metres, right through trees, over lane and ahead by gate, signed to Water End. Follow fence on right then over third stile and along track for 40 metres. Left through gate and diagonally right to field corner opposite group of white houses to right of stream. Right along road to Water End (228043).

Cross A1 and go between garage and café on path signed to Welham Green. (For the swallowhole, continue on road and just past the Woodman, take path on left, also signed to Welham Green. Carry on by side of pub garden, cross an unkempt field full of docks for 300 metres, to come to old oak tree. Here bear right off path and in about 30 metres come to the Swallowhole. To rejoin the original route, return to oak tree and continue on the path past oak 30 metres, turn right and in 15 metres enter next field. Here turn left and in 20 metres cross barbed wire and trespass for about 100 metres by continuing on left side of this field and join original route.) Go by the side of brick garage then across scrubland to enter field with a disused building, Potterells, at the far end, and meet the Swallowhole path. Left along field edge to far corner, where follow path, with stream on left, into trees and soon left over bridge. Across second bridge, over stile and by right edge of field. After 100 metres, over stile and diagonally left across field (30°).

Over stile and right along road. To continue walk, left after 80 metres, between houses numbers 49 and 53 where path signed to 'Bell Bar, 1¼ miles.' For Brookmans Park station, continue along road for 800 metres.

Information

Distance	10½ miles; total 97½ miles. Map 166.
Stations	St Albans City: four an hour, two on Sundays, to St Pancras. Brookmans Park: 3 an hour, half-hourly Sundays, to Kings Cross.
Buses	St Albans to Hatfield: numerous London Country buses. St Albans, Colney Heath, Welham Green, Brookmans Park: 343, hourly, no Sundays.

Bridleway by Oak Farm, nr St Albans
Plough at Smallford

Refreshments   Rose and Crown and two other pubs at Sandridge. The Plough (202070) at Smallford. Colney Heath. Water End café, Old Maypole and Woodman at Water End. Brookmans Park hotel at Brookmans Park.

Accommodation   St Albans (again) or Hatfield.

This stage provides an uneventful country walk with a puzzling wood in the middle and the Lea valley at the end. Shortly after the start at Brookmans Park we need to cross a railway by a level crossing: be very careful, as the crossing is near a bend and the line is the main east coast line with new high speed trains. You may also be in danger from barbarians if southerners are to be believed, as we are just north of the legendary Potters Bar!

The next stretch is across fields which can be very muddy, possibly because the gas mains laid along here spoiled the natural drainage. However, it would always be rather heavy as we are now walking on London clay soil. The path leads on past a whole series of radio aerials at Brookmans Park transmitting station before coming to a quiet stretch of country path again. This starts as a lane and then becomes a path, and then a track, and finally a lane again, and continues for 2½ miles across flat farming country before coming to Newgate Street. This hamlet has two pubs and a restaurant. The Coach and Horses has a large garden and although it is rather twee with its 'Coach Bar' and 'Horse Box', it does have a good stone floor suitable for boots. The Crown is more down to earth; it has a small garden, a large public bar, and food. There is an occasional bus from here to Cuffley or Bayford.

Between Newgate Street and West End the Countryway goes across Wormley Wood. This is a large complicated wood with several small streams, lots of ups and downs, and many different paths. On the map these look very odd, with some being marked as public footpaths and others not acknowledged as such. If you look carefully you will see the ultimate absurdity—an isolated stretch of path with no connection anywhere to the road or other public path! There must clearly be more public rights of way than are marked. Fortunately, people can wander much as they please in the woods, and very pleasant it is, although it is rather easy to get lost. I was lost myself trying to follow two previous sets of directions. As a result the route directions are now rather

lengthy, and to make them easier to follow, the route used is not the most direct way across the wood.

Still, it makes a good walk, and perseverance is rewarded by coming to the Woodman at West End, a small friendly pub which does hot snacks. We can have a rest here before we tackle a last complicated little stretch, caused by the new Wormley bypass and the resulting extinguishment of a good path, to reach the New River at Broxbourne. The New River is a beautiful little canal with green lawn beside it, and built originally to provide water for London. Hugh Myddleton, an alderman of London, with the support of James I set out to provide an additional water supply for London at his own expense. He had a 40-mile channel dug between two springs, at Chadwell and at Amwell near Hertford, and Clerkenwell. The New River was formally opened in 1613 and has carried on providing water for London ever since; although the canal has been shortened and the water supply augmented by water from the river Lea since the eighteenth century. It was owned by the New River Company, and a shareholding in this was very profitable indeed until the canal was taken over by the Metropolitan Water Board in 1904.

Just along the river is St Augustine's parish church at Broxbourne. It was built in the fourteenth and fifteenth centuries, and is a large rather plain-looking church with a long nave with four bays, and north and south arcades. There are a good many monuments in the church, and several interesting brasses. The two oldest tombs are of Sir John Say (1478) and his son Sir William Say, who between them built most of the church. Sir John has a fine tomb of Purbeck marble on which are the effigies of himself and his wife.

Broxbourne station is conveniently close to the church, and has frequent services to Liverpool Street.

Route
From Brookmans Park station, left away from village. Take road signposted to Welham Green and after 800 metres, 50 metres past new Catholic church, right on path between numbers 49 and 53, signposted to Bell Bar, 1¼ miles. Right

Broxbourne Church and New River (146–7)

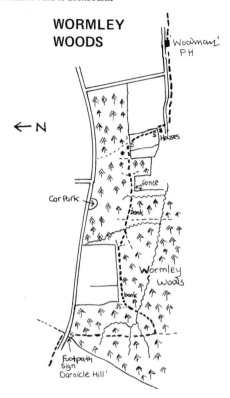

again after 15 metres, and soon through car park and across stream at concrete bridge. Ahead, and later up steps and cross railway. (Be careful!) Ahead across field to join wood on right at end of field. Outside this for 1,000 metres to end at lane bend (253049). Right along lane to A1000. (Pub and transport café 500 metres left). Right along A1000, and left after 160 metres at footpath sign to Grubs Lane. On path between fences, then into field with water tower on right. Follow right edge of field and continue by second field to road (264057).

Right along road, over cross roads and down drive for 800 metres to Barbers Lodge Farm. Go round barn to right, then left through iron gate, and after 20 metres right through iron gate to resume line of travel (130°), and follow hedge on left (273054). Path soon becomes track and keep on through fields. Cross track with Coldharbour Farm on left and keep on to turn where right. Track soon turns sharp left and on to Newgate Street (301050).

Ahead at road junction, past the Gables restaurant and past Coach and Horses on left. Left after 80 metres to Ponsbourne Park Hotel along tarmac drive becoming gravel. Keep ahead and ignore turns off. Left at junction where three silos ahead. Right along road, at drive end. After 700 metres at beginning of Wormley Wood (318066), right along footpath signed to Darnicle Hill.

The next stretch to the Woodman is difficult to follow so take it slowly! Cross stream and in 50 metres at crest of rise follow red-on-white waymarks. Cross second stream, over third stream, and after 80 metres at crest of rise, left along well-used path and leave waymarks. In 200 metres, recross stream, follow track uphill and right along earth bank. Then, with edge of wood on left, continue to end of fields. Here fork right and continue on right till in 200 metres meet wider track and left down to stream. Cross and go right along narrow path. After 50 metres, cross wider path and continue slightly right with earth bank on left (130°). Be careful here: the first wider path also has an earth bank on its left, rather more conspicuous at the start than the one we want. Cross stream and in 50 metres reach corner of wire fence. Carry on this path, or a parallel path on left when it gets overgrown, until you come to wire fence and field on right.

Continue to stile into field. Cross stile and head down field to far left corner, over stile, and by narrow path by house to squeeze gate and lane. Left, and keep on for 600 metres to Woodman on right (338060). (Alternatively, we can avoid all difficulties to here, but have much more road-walking, by continuing on the road past the path to Darnicle Hill for 1,000 metres until 100 metres past road on left, right into woods at a footpath signed to West End. On for 150 metres till at clear cross tracks, left 50 metres, right 150 metres and reach stile into fields as in original route.)

Keep on and in 400 metres, just beyond road on right, take track on left between hedges and trees. After the track joins a drive and past a new house, right through gate and along right edge of field by dog-leg to SE. corner. Over barbed wire to lane (348066), right at road junction, left along Spring Walk. Fifty metres on, at bend, right over stile. Along right edge of field (Lea Valley ahead). Over stile at bottom, then over footbridge and left along stream to stile, 50 metres to right of stream in new fence ahead. Right by fence and at end left on road, then right over bridge over motorway (359068).

Right at far side along track to second field-gate opposite path on west side of motorway. Left down between hedges to join lane. Cross New River to join A10 at Broxbourne (366063). Cross road, left to New River bridge, right through kissing gate and on path beside river.

At Broxbourne church, right down Mill Lane to Lea Valley Regional Park, toilets and camping area. Left through car park, cross bridge over stream, then on left of little field and under railway line. (For Broxbourne station, before this railway line, go on path under large railway bridge, through station car park and up steps on left to station. Café on left over bridge and pub by station.) To continue walk, right by side of rail line with car park on left. Up to road, cross bridge, and past L.V.R.P. boat centre.

Information

Distance $11\frac{1}{2}$ miles; total 109 miles. Map 166.

Stations Brookmans Park, Bayford, Cuffley: all 3 an hour, half-hourly Sundays, to Kings Cross.
Broxbourne: half-hourly to Liverpool St.

Buses London Country 308, Hertford, Bayford Station, Newgate Street, Cuffley station: four-hourly Monday–Saturday. No Sunday service.

Refreshments Bell Bar transport café (252054). The Crown, and Coach and Horses at Newgate Street. Woodman at West End, good soups (338060). Café by station and several pubs at Broxbourne.

Accommodation Harlow Youth Hostel, Hertford, Ware.

This is a fascinating section, with long stretches of two
entirely different parks: the new Lea Valley Regional Park in
the first half, and East London's country retreat, Epping
Forest, in the second half. To add still more interest, the
magnificent Waltham Abbey lies between.

The walk starts at Broxbourne and keeps by the river for
four miles to reach Waltham Abbey. This section arouses
quite different reactions among walkers: some find it dull and
rather ugly with its stretches of rather boring canal bank,
flooded gravel pits, and views of electricity pylons. Others,
including myself, think it a watery parkland with hosts of
different birds, hidden backwaters and subtly changing
patterns of water and scenery. You will be able to discover
which view you agree with. One group to whom the attraction
is obvious is fishermen—and some fisherwomen—whom you
will find in abundance along the whole stretch of river, no
matter what the weather. I have walked it on a day of
torrential rain and floods, but the fishers were still there, some
in little polythene tents but others under just umbrellas.

In the past the Lea was a busy commercial river, after the
Lea Navigation was made and its shoals cleared in 1739. In
1765 new cuts were made and a continuous navigation route
was established. But by the 1950s the area had run down
badly; the glass house industry was decaying, and its remains,
plus numerous reservoirs and the electricity pylons, did not
make it too attractive. However, a number of people saw the
potential of the Lea Valley, which flows from Ware and goes
by some of the densest packed housing in London—
Walthamstow, Leytonstone, and Hackney. These were all
short of space for outdoor recreation, and though the Lea
went right through the area with its great possibilities, it was
used very little.

Illtyd Harrington, at the time of writing deputy leader of
the Labour group on the G.L.C., campaigned for the area to
be renovated, and after an Act of Parliament was passed the
Lea Valley Regional Park Authority (L.V.R.P.A.) was set up
in 1966.

Its objective is not to create an urban park with pretty flower beds, but to keep a semi-rural atmosphere with lots of scope for outdoor activities. There is a marina at Stanstead Abbots, near Ware, which hires out cabin cruisers; there are good facilities for horse-riding and cycling on a cycle circuit. Two reservoirs have been opened for sailing, and the Picketts Lock Centre near Edmonton has a sports and leisure centre for more informal recreation. Broxbourne Lido, opened in 1978, has an artificial wave machine and a solarium.

At the start of this section of the walk at Broxbourne there is a camp site and chalets for hire. There are also one or two backwaters with waterlilies, and grass to picnic on. Refreshment places are plentiful, with a café and pubs at Broxbourne, and a collection of pubs and cafés, including one Chinese, at Cheshunt. There is also a tea place right beside the canal at Cheshunt Lock, where flasks may be filled. Just

before Waltham Abbey, where we join the road, is another pub, the Old English Gentleman.

Waltham Abbey is a small town with some interesting buildings in the Market Square, but some with rather run-down property nearby, which may improve now that that the main traffic load bypasses the town. The name Waltham means 'forest homestead' and in the middle ages Epping Forest was known as Waltham Forest. In the Domesday Book forty-seven and a half plough teams and 2,382 swine were recorded as being kept in the forest. Early in the eleventh century a holy cross was found through a vision at Montacute in Somerset, and Tofig the Proud, Cnut's standard bearer, built a church in Waltham to house it. The church was rebuilt and richly endowed by King Harold for secular canons, and Harold was probably buried here after the battle of Hastings. Later, Henry II converted the college into an Abbey to expiate his murder of Thomas à Becket. No expense was spared, and two hundred and sixty-five cartloads of lead were supposed to have been used for the roof.

Most of this building was destroyed at the dissolution of the monasteries, when Waltham Abbey was the last to surrender to Henry VIII, in 1540. Fortunately, 30 metres of the nave were saved for use as the parish church. Excavations show that 100 metres have disappeared, so the original abbey must have been very large. Even the surviving church dominates the town and has given its name to it.

The abbey site is behind the church, and is bare of remains except for a brief vaulted passage, gateway and bridge. It has now been leased by the L.V.R.P.A. and made into a picnic area for visitors. There are several old walls which divide up the area, a small mill-stream, a rose garden and an old orchard with several bench seats. Despite the rumble of traffic on the bypass, it is very peaceful just to sit here under the apple trees and gaze at the rear of the church.

The church is a rebuilding of the 1100s, with the west front built in 1315, the west tower in 1550, and the top storey in 1905. Inside, the church gives an impression of splendour and magnificence. The great walls of the nave, plain as can be,

Sailing on the Lea, nr Cheshunt

form the perfect frame for the brilliantly painted ceiling, the carved east wall and the beautiful stained glass windows. The ceiling is a copy of the original Norman ceiling of Peterborough, and was painted by E. J. Poynter in the nineteenth century. The east wall was remodelled and carved by William Burges. The reredos, which separated the old Abbey church from the parish church, was carved with gilded scenes of the Nativity by W. G. Nichol. The windows are the most brilliant feature of the church and are one of the most glorious productions of the Pre-Raphaelites, with the brilliant blues and flame colours of Burne-Jones.

There is also a splendid wall-painting in a chapel at the side, and a small stone figure of about 1400, the Waltham Abbey Madonna, found in a garden nearby in 1974. In the crypt there is an interesting little exhibition by the Waltham Abbey historical society, which includes a genealogical table for King Harold. The society also runs a museum in Sun Street, open at week-ends.

Outside the church a long black and white timber-framed range of buildings, including the Welsh Harp, separates the churchyard from Market Square. There is a record of a market being held here in 1189, and certainly one has taken place on Tuesdays ever since 1560. A shop in the square has timbers carved by medieval artists, showing a woman with a jug. North of the main road, at the end of Powder Mill Lane, there was an explosives factory from the Civil War until 1943. Waltham has several pubs including the interesting-looking Bakers Arms, and two or three cafés, including a Chinese one. Blunk's, a very expensive restaurant, is also available if you feel like making a splash.

From the Abbey the route goes by the side of rather an industrial area, and then by the side of a Ministry of Defence establishment. The London orbital motorway, Ringway 3 or the M16/25, is planned to go through here and then across our route to go by Upshire round Epping. It was contested vigorously by local people assisted by John Tyme, but the scales were weighted heavily against them.

Our route goes by the side of a small new housing estate and then into the country again by field paths. It is a little

View over Epping Forest from High Beach

complicated at the start, but we eventually reach High Beach. The motorway will run across the playing fields, but there will a footbridge across it. There will obviously be much disruption to our route, when it is built, but I hope it will still be peaceful once away from the immediate scene. The result would make quite a contrast to the view Tennyson had, who lived at High Beach Park from 1837–40.

High Beach itself is a small scattered village with a church buried in the trees. The route passes the Duke of Wellington pub and the Epping Forest Youth Hostel on the other side. This is a simple hostel, open daily in summer, but only week-ends during the rest of the year. It is superbly situated right opposite an open glade and facing directly on to the forest.

There is a rough lane by the side of the hostel, and down it there used to be a pub called Turpin's Cave, but it is now a private house and not open to the public. Dick Turpin was born in Hempstead, on the Suffolk border. He started as a butcher's apprentice and lived near Epping in Sewardstone. Later, after he had turned highwayman and his address had become known, he hid in a cave in the forest at High Beach,

thought to have been the one in the grounds of this house. Relics of his were supposed to have been found there, and were on display in the public house, but these have gone now that the pub has closed.

Back on the route, and about 300 metres past the hostel, we come to the Royal Oak Inn. This is a big old rambling pub, with lots of bars, a games room, and bar billiards—ideal for the noisy extrovert. No food appears to be served there, however. Behind the inn is the Epping Forest Conservation Centre, with an exhibition and public information desk, open every day except Monday and Tuesday. Our route goes beside the centre, and we stay in the forest for about another 4 miles. Sometimes the forest is quite dense, but mostly there are large trees—hornbeams and beeches—in open glades. There is considerable variety, from lovely little paths with high banks to muddy well-used horse rides. The forest is frequented by a lot of people and is looked after by the Epping Forest Conservators; but one can still go for a long period without seeing anyone, except when crossing the roads that intersect the forest. The main area of the forest lies between Epping and Chingford, but narrower strips penetrate right into London to end at Wanstead Flats. A good walk about 10 miles long may be made from here to Epping, keeping to the forest all the way.

This was preserved for us all by the efforts of one old man who lived in Loughton in the last century. The forest area had been diminished over the years by enclosures and development: the local vicar decided to enclose more of the forest, and had a fence erected to keep out the villagers who used to go into the forest to lop wood. On the traditional opening day, Thomas Willingale stuck by local custom and led his sons into the area and asserted his rights 'in common' to lop wood. He was summoned and jailed for his temerity by the local magistrates, who, as so often, acted in the interests of the local gentry. Willingale's action and his imprisonment brought in the Commons Preservation Society and, later, the City of London, as owners of some of the forest. The case was fought in the courts for fifteen years, but was only settled by

Old tree in Epping Forest

the Epping Forest Act of 1878. In this Act the City of London Corporation was appointed 'conservator of the forest'. Part of the settlement was the extinguishment of the original lopping rights, but in compensation £7,000 was given by the city to Loughton to build Lopping Hall with reading- and lecture-rooms. All ended happily, but it took years of struggle and one obstinate man to achieve it. Many of our liberties that are taken for granted have needed 'direct action' and 'unreasonable people' who would stand on principle. The courts and 'sticking to the law' have been of little value on their own.

We can argue about this while walking in the forest and enjoying those freedoms. On the route we pass Ambersbury Banks, an old iron-age fort stretching over twelve acres. There is a 2-metre rampart, 700 metres round, with a ditch 3 metres deep and 6 metres across. It is grown over by trees and, despite its size, can be missed. Keep close to the road at about the right point to make sure of seeing it.

After this, we go by lesser paths to Theydon Bois. This is a large village with shops, pubs which do food, a pleasant village green and a Victorian church. This has some interesting hatchments—coats of arms of the deceased— including a rare one of James I. There is also a memorial window to Miss Buss, the pioneer of women's secondary education and founder of the North London Collegiate school for girls. Her grave is in the churchyard outside, and well visited.

Route

From Broxbourne station, left along Station Road, left down steps to lower station car park, right under iron road-bridge, left on path by rail line, over little bridge over stream, left on tunnel under line, right on path and left to road. Right along road, past L.V.R.P. boat centre and ahead on tow path by Lea Navigation. After 2 miles pass Cheshunt Lock and small tea place, and 4 miles from Broxbourne, at Waltham, go under road bridge, then up by pub, the Old English Gentleman, to road and right along road to Waltham Abbey. Continue on right-hand road, and then after Market Square,

right on Sewardstone Street and left on Greenfield Street
to reach the main road. Right, then left on Denny Ave and
down alley way at end to Elm Close. Here turn right on little
tarmac path by stream past backs of houses, to reach playing
fields. Left past back of swimming baths and then right across
playing field (soon to be by bridge over M25) to the houses at
end of Lodge Lane.

Continue to end, then, just past the last houses, turn right
on track for 300 metres, then left by little stream for 100
metres, right on track 150 metres by edge of field, then follow
track left across field. Then on right of hedge, right for 200
metres and left over stile. Keep on same direction with hedge
on left following a succession of fields to reach road. Left on
road 100 metres then right on road, Wellington Hill.

Continue on past Youth Hostel and Duke of Wellington to
road, and, in 100 metres, meet second road at Kings Oak
Hotel (toilets). Pass left of pub on small road and where this
bends right, keep ahead on trail into trees (130°) with fence on
right.

Meet sandy lane and follow to right for 50 metres, and
then left and in 150 metres down to road on A11. Cross
carefully to small parking space (415980). Ahead on track just
to right of sign (130°) for 600 metres to cross track. Turn left
down sandy track and north for 1 mile to A121. Cross half-
left and into parking space. Follow sandy track to right, later
left behind area, and then swing right downhill to small
bridge. Ahead uphill to wide crossing track, 150 metres past
top of rise where left, and in 600 metres reach road (B172).
Cross at car parking area and resume sandy track (10°).

Continue on track for 900 metres to reach Ambersbury
Banks earthworks on the left. Leave main track here and go
right by a small ditch/stream (100°) to reach stream junction.
Left along this stream for 600 metres, following a path after a
while, to reach wider sandy cross-track. Right along this, over
stream bridge and pass golf course on left. Continue for 300
metres to wide junction at paths.

Carry on in same direction just to right of wire fence and
backs of house until after 600 metres reach open space with
football pitch. Cross half left to road, then left for 800 metres

on road, passing church on left and keeping 'Bull' on right, to
reach Theydon Bois station.

Information

Distance	11 miles, total 120 miles. Maps 166 and 167.
Stations	Broxbourne, Cheshunt, Waltham Cross: half-hourly, to Liverpool Street. Theydon Bois, Loughton: Central undergound line.
Buses	Numerous till Waltham Abbey. London Transport, 20, Epping to Loughton on A121. London Country 329, Waltham Cross to Epping, hourly. No Sunday service.
Admission	Waltham Abbey museum, 41 Sun Street, free. Saturday 10 a.m.–4 p.m. Sunday 3–5 p.m. Epping Forest Information Centre (tel. 01 413 981), free. Wednesday–Saturday, 10 a.m.–12.30 p.m. and 2–5.30 p.m. Sunday 11 a.m.–12.30 p.m. and 2–5.30p.m.
Refreshments	Cheshunt Lock, tea and tea flasks filled. Cafés and pubs at Cheshunt. Old English Gentleman (375005). Pubs and cafés at Waltham Abbey. Duke of Wellington (408983), Royal Oak (412981), and tea hut there. Pubs at Theydon Bois.
Accommodation	Epping Youth Hostel, Chingford, Epping, Loughton, Woodford.

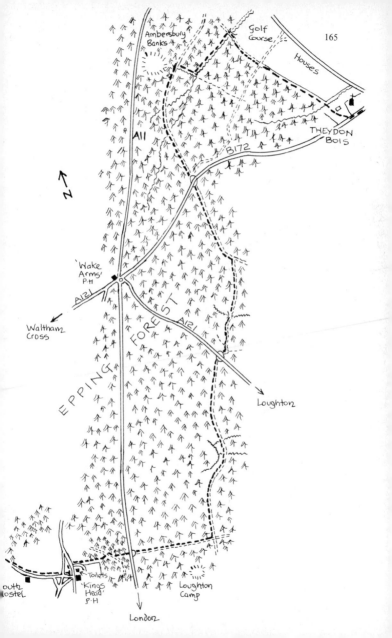

Ambersbury Banks

Golf Course

Houses

A11

B172

THEYDON BOIS

N

'Wake Arms' P.H

A121

Waltham Cross

A121

EPPING FOREST

Loughton

outh Hostel

Toilets

'Kings Head' P.H

Loughton Camp

London

This stage gives a quiet country walk by little-used paths going from church to church across the Essex upland. These churches are now isolated with either no apparent congregation or only small groups of cottages, but they are all worth looking at. In addition, only 2 miles off the route is the unique wooden Saxon church at Greensted. If all are to be seen, a day will not be too long—with the paths being on London clay, and a little hard to follow.

The route of the M25 in this area has now been confirmed and, to take the Countryway further from this, the first mile of this section, to the M11, is new since the first edition. There is a pleasant footpath stretch from Theydon Bois until we go under the M11 just south of the intended interchange with the M25.

From the M11 we go uphill to Theydon Garnon church, which makes a handsome picture from the slope. This is reasonably old with the tower being built in 1520, and the brick north aisle in 1644.

After the church, there is a long, straight, wide green track of about 1 mile along the course of an old Roman road, where there is a planned crossing over the projected M25. The route then goes along a road in front of Hill Hall, a remarkable Elizabethan Renaissance building begun by Thomas Smith in 1577. It has many features of Italian and French buildings that appealed to him, particularly the giant Tuscan columns in the courtyard. There are also wall-paintings done in the 1570s showing the story of Cupid and Psyche. However, these cannot be seen, as Hill Hall is an open prison for women—and thus not open to the public!

You may have some views of the exterior going across the fields to Stapleford Tawney church, and from the road near there. The church is old, with the chancel built in 1220, and the nave and the south chapel soon after. It was drastically restored in the 1860s and, after a fire in the 1960s, was renovated and restored again. There are two stone coffins dating from the twelfth century, one near the south porch, and the other outside on the north side. The church is now plain inside, although there is some attractive exposed wood in the belfry. The absence of stained glass, the views of the trees outside and the light airy nature of the interior make this a very peaceful place to sit in and rest. It is also left open, which is a change hereabouts.

Next, there are paths in really rural surroundings, by the back of woods and along the hedgerows, but they are sometimes difficult to find, until we come to the A113 and two roadside pubs, the Woodman, and the White Bear. These are good places to stop and have a snack before making a diversion to Greensted church near Chipping Ongar. This church is two miles off the route, but unless you are pressed for time, it is a detour that should be made, to see the only wooden church in the country remaining from Saxon times. It is probably the oldest wooden church in the world.

The church has three sections: the tower, the wooden nave, and a brick chancel, all quite different but blending in with each other. The nave is the Saxon part, with low walls made of oak split down the middle and placed vertically, round side outwards. These walls had to be restored in 1848 when the rotting bottom portions of oak were cut off and replaced by a low brick pediment and the remainder of the timber placed on this so that the church remained at the same height. They are blackened with age now, as well they might be, for the timbers have been tested and found to belong to the year 845.

The earliest church on the site, in the clearing in the great Essex forest, was built around the seventh century, and is thought to have been enlarged in the year 845 to form the wooden Saxon church still here. The wooden timbers have since been tongued and grooved on the flat side to keep out draughts. The brick chancel was rebuilt on Norman flat footings about 1500. The deep red brick, the priest's doorway, and the west window are all beautiful, but spiritually overshadowed by the simple wooden nave. Inside, this is cool, dark and solemn, with low oak beams, and gives the feeling that this must have been how the early Christains experienced

Roman road at Hobbs Cross
Stapleford Tawney Church

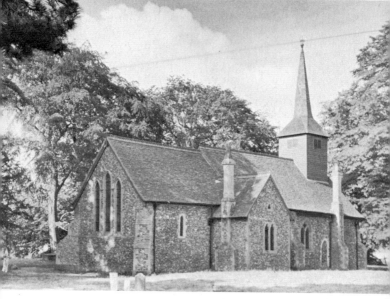

the church. It is the last remaining shrine of one of the very few Saxon saints, St Edmund. Edmund, king of the East Saxons, was killed by the Danes in 870. His body is said to have rested here before burial at Bury St Edmunds.

Greensted is also the place where later English martyrs, the Tolpuddle martyrs, lived for a period. Public outcry and agitation succeeded in bringing the Tolpuddle martyrs, those early trade unionists, back from their transportation to Australia, but was not powerful enough to overcome the prejudice of local land owners. They could not get employment in Dorset, and were resettled in Greensted before their final move to Canada. While they were living in Greensted, one, James Brine, married Elizabeth Standfield, the daughter of one of his fellow martyrs, and the marriage is recorded in the parish register. The atmosphere here was apparently more congenial than in Dorset.

Back on our route, at the White Bear, we cross the river
Roding by a large bridge. Unfortunately the route on this
low-lying stretch can sometimes be impassable in winter from
flooding, when we have to go round by the road instead. The
whole Roding valley is an attractive one, but is perhaps more
so in its upper reaches than here. About 1 mile the other side
of the river, after a long stretch across a field—once a park—
we come to another isolated church beside one or two houses,
with its own little set of trees. This church is called St Thomas
the Apostle, at Navestock. It has a needle-sharp spire, and is a
very large church for such a small collection of houses—it is,
indeed, now combined with the church at Kelvedon Hatch,
under one vicar. However, the parish, by its own efforts,
managed in fifteen years to have the church thoroughly
restored and repaired, after it had been badly damaged by a
landmine falling in the churchyard in 1940. The end result
justifies the effort. The church has traces of eleventh-century
work in the west and north walls, but the tower and spire,
erected in the fifteenth century, were of sufficient strength to
withstand the 1940 bomb! Inside, the church has big old oak
beams, with some stonework, little niches with statues (more
ornate than in many other churches), a new organ and redstone
cracked flags made from old gravestones. There is a sense of
space and airiness about the church which made it good to sit
in after a walk across the hot Essex fields.

There is a pleasant stroll after this, though with an obscure
path from the road to Navestock Side. There is a good green
here where village cricket is played right opposite the Green
Man pub. There is then one obstruction, a wide unbridged
ditch to try to get across, and another short stretch before the
end of the walk at Bentley. This church was also damaged in
the war by a German rocket in 1945, but is otherwise not
particularly interesting.

There is an hourly bus from here to Brentwood (rather less
frequent on Sundays), but the Countryway route is only three
miles and so easy to follow (I hope) that you may prefer to
carry on to Brentwood station to finish there. However, to
keep distances reasonable and not to have mileages too

Greensted Church

uneven, I have finished this stage here and continue the
description in the next section.

Route

Leave Theydon Bois station by a footbridge from the station
yard over the railway. Then left by a footpath on the east side,
over a stile, through fields and along a tarmac drive until just
before a gate into a sports field, Here, right over a stile,
keeping stream on the left; over a second stile, and continue
across the next field in the same direction (80°) to an isolated
stile in the middle of the field. Then go slightly left to corner
of field at edge of trees. Over small ditch and continue with
trees and ditch on left. Continue on left edge of field, over
plank bridge and stile into another field and keep along right
edge of this field (100°) to barn. (Do not take left stile.)
Continue over stile into track, right on track and through
tunnel under the M11 (468997). Follow small path just to the
left of little stream and over bridge and stile into field facing
Theydon Garnon church. Head up field (140°) to stile to right
of church and on to farm lane to pass Theydon Garnon
church on right. Left at road, and at T-junction, Hobbs Cross
Farm, continue ahead through gap and down a green lane for
1,500 metres under pylon wires and between hedgerows. The
M25 is planned to cross this path but there should be a
crossing. At end at gate, keep on along lane for 150 metres to
road and telephone box (485004).

Here turn right uphill. Ignore a footpath sign on the left,
and continue round a right-hand bend. 20 metres after passing
the drive to Hill Hall on your right, and when the fence on the
left ends, turn half-left across a large field, aiming for the
second electricity pole to left of the farm. Pass through a
hurdle gate and continue in the same direction to fence in the
far corner, which cross and follow the line of electricity poles
to a stile in the hedge ahead. Here turn half-right to cross the
wire by an electricity pole about 50 metres to the right of a
small wood (do not go over stile into wood), follow edge of
wood for 100 metres, then right across field (140°) and aim for
church ahead in trees under pylon wires. Enter churchyard
through gate in corner and walk on with Stapleford Tawney

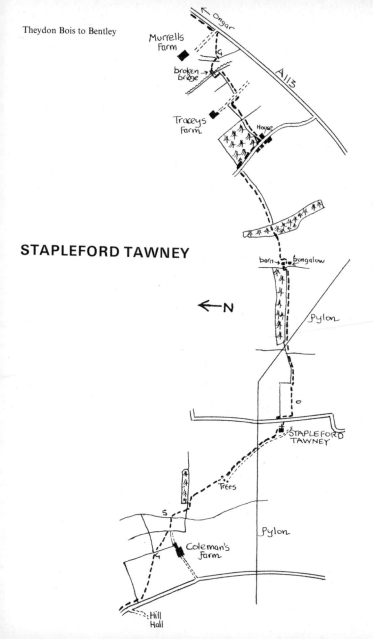

Theydon Bois to Bentley

Ongar

A113

Murrells Farm

G

broken bridge

Traceys Farm

House

STAPLEFORD TAWNEY

← N

barn → bungalow

Pylon

0

STAPLEFORD TAWNEY

Trees

S

Pylon

Coleman's Farm

Hill Hall

church on your left to a little lane, water tap on right at exit gate (502990).

Right along road for 70 metres, then left into field opposite Great Tawney Hall. Straight across field (100°) and soon join hedge on left. Ahead along right edge of wood and under pylons in second field. At field end, left into wood for 20 metres, then right and go between barn and bungalow. Swing left behind barn, then right across field via trees. Ahead through wood and at far side over fence, horse-gated. Ahead over field with hedge on right. Right along lane for 200 metres, then left into field just before house on left (522992). (You may need to go right of house to get on to the path.)

The next stage has rather more barbed wire than should be, so be careful. Ahead along left edge of this and next field to Traceys Farm Lane. Right for 100 metres, then left along field edge. Left at stream for 30 metres and cross near ruined wood bridge. Bear right (110°) over field and barbed fence. Through gate and left across field and over stile to road. Left along verge of A113 for 500 metres and past the Woodman on right. Then swing down right to the White Bear (532998).

Right along footpath with sign, on left of pub, soon over stile and on between fences. Over footbridge and half-left (150°) to gap ahead in trees. (This stretch is liable to flooding: if it is, the alternative is a long way by the A113 to 522987, then by minor road to Navestock Hall 540982.) At gap follow track on right alongside stream through field. Keep ahead on track for 800 metres to Navestock Hall Farm. Through farm with church on left. On down to road and left for 800 metres, past a right and left turn. Just after a narrow belt of trees comes in from left and track enters field on right (545978), go left over loose barbed-wire fence and immediately right by hedge and into field next to road. Follow left edge of field with stream on left. Cross ditch via bridge to second field and then by bridge over stream in this field. Then after 100 metres, right over stream into trees. Follow green lane to end and take middle exit into field. Left along edge of fields until white house is reached, the Green Man. Ahead across green and slight right (140°) to gap in hedge. Cross two fields (145°) heading just to right of Radio Tower ahead via gaps in hedges. Jump or scramble over a bridgeless ditch! Half-left over third field (150°) to blue house. Follow track to lane and junction with A128 (567969). A bus can be caught from here to Brentwood.

To continue walk, or to get to Brentwood station by path, right along lane and follow Countryway directions in next section.

Information

Distance	9½ miles; total 129½ miles. Maps 177 or 167.
Stations	Theydon Bois: Central Line. Brentwood: twenty-minute intervals to Liverpool St.
Buses	Epping, Kelvedon Hatch, Brentwood: London Country 339. Pilgrims Hatch to Brentwood: London Country 339 and Eastern National 260 about every 2 hours on Sunday.
Refreshments	Woodman, White Bear (hot and cold snacks) 532999. Green Man, Alma Arms (curries, Irish stew, no food Sundays) at Navestock Side. Several cafés and pubs near station at Brentwood.
Accommodation	Epping Forest Youth Hostel, Brentwood, Kelvedon Hatch, Romford.

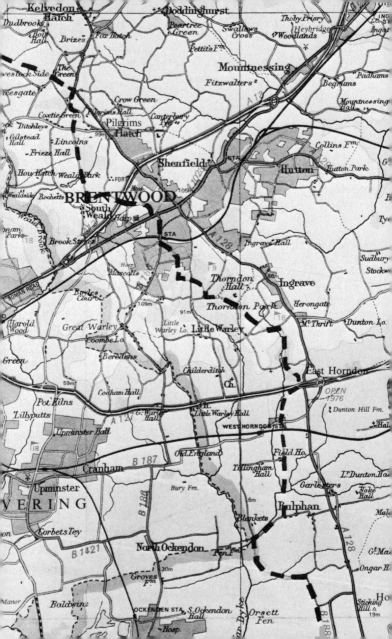

This stage is quite different from earlier ones, with little true countryside but with two large and contrasting country parks instead. There is also a 2-mile stretch of road between them, the longest on the entire route. A glance on the map will show the difficulty. Without going right round Brentwood, and missing the two parks, there is no real alternative—though several were tried. The gap between Romford and Brentwood is planned to take the M16/M25 motorway, and there are no public paths anyway!

The walk starts from Bentley, with a good uphill path, but one that needs careful following to reach the road near Coxtie Green. The Alma Arms here does pleasant pub food, with curries and Irish stew, except on Sundays. Across the road is an enclosed path which leads into the Weald Park. There is a wood at the start with occasional picnic tables, but the rest is wide open parkland leading down to a fair-sized lake, with ducks and fishermen. The other side of the lake is again open parkland, but with many more people, and the scene can become quite crowded at week-ends. Fortunately, the park is big enough to accommodate them as well as those visitors seeking more solitude.

Just to the right, out of the park, is the hamlet of South Weald, a pleasing little place. There is a village shop and post office, the Tower Arms, an eighteenth-century free house, and, round the corner, the fifteenth-century Golden Fleece Inn. The church is a large medieval building with a Norman doorway and sixteenth-century tower, but, heavily restored by the Victorians. It is rather gloomy inside and is best known as the place where the infamous Lord Chief Justice Scroggs is buried. He was appointed Chief Justice by Charles II, and was responsible for prosecuting, judging and sentencing to death the alleged conspirators caught up in the accusations of Titus Oates.

After South Weald we have our 2 miles of road. But even this is interesting, if you note the gradual change of character, from a country ride at the start to a busy commercial street near Brentwood station. There are useful shops of all kinds here, with several cafés, pubs, a fish and chip shop, take-away food shops (not Sundays), and a good camping and walking equipment shop. There is a very good train service from the station, so you are unlikely to need to explore Brentwood to use up time—there is little to tempt you to, except for two old coaching inns, the White Hart, with a fine coaching yard, and the Chequers. Brentwood was a good stop for coaches before the coming of the railway in 1846.

After a few back roads, we come surprisingly quickly from the station to woodland, and can, if we wish, stay in woods for virtually all the rest of this stage. Even at the start the woods are quiet, and they remove one from the town almost immediately. There are 1,200 metres of this birch wood thickly covered with brambles before we reach the entrance to Thorndon Park. This is another large park made up from a series of acquisitions over a period of years. It is 2½ miles long and has two distinct portions, the North Park and the South Park, which are joined by a narrow strip of path. The North Park is a birch wood, but is rather less thickly covered than the earlier woods and has several clearings, some with tables and benches for picnickers. There are separate tracks for horse-riding, and an innovation here that could well be copied elsewhere: to try to prevent the damage that comes from riders using footpaths, a permit system has been introduced. People wishing to ride have to obtain a permit, usable in both Thorndon Park and Weald Park, and wear a numbered armband. This allows people to note any rider not sticking to the horse tracks, and those responsible to be banned.

The route goes down the main drive which cars use. You may avoid them by making a beeline through the woods, but if you do, keep a close watch on your direction as it is rather easy to lose yourself! Near where we leave the northern half of the park, you will see on the map a church buried in the woodland, south west of Thorndon Hall. You may be able to pick your way through the woods to find this and discover a little mausoleum and chantry chapel, designed by Pugin. It has delicate window tracery, with angels leaning over the west door, and scenes of the Crucifixion, Burial and Resurrection

East Horndon Church

under the east window. Part of Thorndon Hall, for which it was built, is now used as a club house for Thorndon Hall Golf Club.

The path between the two halves of the park goes beside the golf course, and gives excellent views over the Essex plain, with its industrial chimneys, to the Kent hills beyond. This path is also much quieter than the main portions of the park, not that these are crowded on weekdays. The southern park has some woodland and a lake hidden among the trees, but is altogether more open. And we have more good views from 30 metres or so above the level at this side of the Thames.

The Brentwood to Tilbury road has now been moved to the east of the way shown on older maps, to go on a flyover over the Southend Road. Between the new road and the old road is East Horndon church, on a little knoll. This can be approached direct across the grassland which is part of the park. It is squat, with two storeys, but stands out well above

the prevailing flatness. The chancel and south transept are fifteenth-century on the site of a thirteenth-century church; and the south chapel, porch and tower, were added in the sixteenth century. Inside, the church contains several monuments to the Tyrells of Heron Hall, notably one dated 1442 to Alice Tyrell in an elaborately canopied niche, flanked by her children with their names on scrolls. There is another by Nollekens, dated 1776. The church was neglected for years until it passed into the care of the Redundant Churches Fund in 1972. Since then it has been restored by volunteers and is now open on summer weekends.

At the old crossing of the A128 with the A127 is a collection of refreshment places on both sides of the road. This looks difficult to cross with so many lanes of traffic, but is in fact easier than where the road is not dualled. The Halfway House is a large pub, where trade has obviously decreased since the new road, but it is to be recommended. It is a free house and serves a good selection of ales, including Youngs, and does appetizing snacks and lunchtime meals which, at the times I have been there, were cheaper than in the Little Chef next door. There are also two cafés on the other side of the road, which seem to offer good value.

There is a last short, rather dull, section to West Horndon, where there is a good train service to London, and a bus service to Romford. There are also reasonable pubs in the village, and a restaurant, Le Gourmet, which does not seem too expensive. This stage ends at West Horndon, but if you started at Brentwood, you may wish to continue to Orsett, the next place with convenient public transport.

Route

From Brentwood station, take a bus to Pilgrims Hatch and get off at Bentley at a bend in the A128 (567969). Here left along lane and right at T-junction after 100 metres. On past church on right and after 70 metres, left down a track, footpath 13. 50 metres on, right down footpath 14 to right of fence. Over stile then on short enclosed path through a gate and half-right over field to a gate (170°). Then head to right of

Thorndon Park

a white house and cross two more fields to lane by right of the house. Ahead, over road and along dirt lane, footpath 17. Soon go through swing gate into the Weald Country Park (569954). On along path for 900 metres, ignoring all crossing paths. Pass to left of lake, going through swing gate, across stream and on uphill with fence on right. Toilets (and water tap) are on the right at top of hill. Here left at pond. Right after 200 metres, through gate and left along road (575940).

On for 1¼ miles over A12 to traffic lights and continue down to roundabout. Go on past Brentwood station and take the third left past station, Avenue Road, later called Headley Chase.

At T-junction at end, go left and in 100 metres right along Guardsman Close, with footpath sign at beginning. Continue on footpath at end into wood. Left at T-junction of paths to road. Cross road and then right on path, just inside wood on

the other side of road. Along path for 200 metres with bank on right, then right on planks over ditch and continue left along a path with a ditch, and later fence on left to come out on road opposite entrance to Thorndon Park.

Go through gates and follow drive to end (651911) at sign to Hatch House and Farm. (Alternatively, head from entrance across woodland on the bearing 130°.) Do not go there, but swing left to squeeze gate then right over stile, footpath to Herongate. The path continues between fences with a wood, then a golf course, on the left. The path later crosses a stream and bears left, still keeping the golf course on the left. Just inside woods, path comes to a T-junction at a path sign. Take left-hand path, and 200 metres on at end of wood right at stile. Then along path 41 to lake. Bear right, keeping lake on right, and at end of lake, at cross tracks by water tap, left up hard track to go to the right of octagonal wood, toilets. Then bear diagonally right down across grassland, heading a little to right of church. At the road, the old A128, right down to the Halfway House. Cross A127 and right along it.

Pass Woodside Farm and then left into field after next belt of trees. Ahead along left edge, over stile, follow right edge of next field and ahead to road. Across road and along path 41. At the next road, right for 300 metres for West Horndon station. (To continue with walk, go left instead for 100 metres and then right on path between houses 117 and 119, signposted to Bulphan.)

Information

Distance	9 miles; total 138½ miles. Map 177.
Stations	Brentwood: twenty-minute intervals to Liverpool Street. West Horndon: half-hourly to Fenchurch Street.

Buses   London Country 339 and Eastern National
260 to Pilgrims Hatch, about three an hour
on weekdays and two hourly on Sundays.
Eastern National 26 Basildon to Romford
via Halfway House and West Horndon,
hourly. No Sunday service. Eastern
National 265 Brentwood to West
Horndon, once in four hours, none
Sundays.

Refreshments   Ice creams normally at Weald Park and at
South Weald. Tower Arms and Golden
Fleece at South Weald. Cafés, pubs and
take-away food shops at Brentwood.
Halfway House pub, good food and two
cafés opposite on A127 (633893). Le
Gourmet restaurant, lunches and dinners,
except on Mondays, refreshment stall at
station and pubs at West Horndon.

Accommodation   Brentwood, Bulphan.

This stage, across the flat Essex coastal plain, gives a new experience, with the fields seeming to stretch on forever, the numerous dykes, and the wide skyscapes. It can be desolate in an east wind with rain or snow, but with the sun shining it is a pastoral delight. What is not so delightful is the gluey nature of the London clay over which the route runs, and the quality of many of the footpaths—one has to persevere to get across some of the ploughed fields, where it sometimes seems the path has never been used! The Ramblers Association is working to get these better marked, and regular use by such as the London Countryway will help considerably. Despite appearances, the route chosen does use some of the better established paths! The effort should be worth while, however, for the historic places on the way.

The start of the route is by a clearly signposted path, and goes in a straight line, with occasional changes over ditches, to a narrow road. Along here is an isolated public house, the Harrow, which offers limited food. This is the closest we approach to Greater London on the whole route, being only 300 metres away from the boundary. The route continues on a good track by the side of the pub, but this gradually fades away. There is then a difficult stretch to follow, with two dykes to cross, one without a bridge, and a good deal of ploughed field. You will be relieved to come out on another little lane and have the going easier for a while, while walking towards the great block of Orsett hospital ahead.

Just before entering the village, you pass on the right the site of a 'motte and bailey' marked on the map. The motte is 200 metres across but all that can be seen from the path is a ditch. On the same site are the remains of a building said to be Bishop Bonner's palace. Bonner was Bishop of London in the mid 1500s, was dismissed in Edward VI's reign, but reinstated by Mary. He was in charge of the persecution of Protestants in Essex and had many burnt at the stake. He was dismissed again by Elizabeth and ended his life in prison. At first glance, Orsett itself has only its great new hospital and a number of pleasant but ordinary new houses, but round corners and partly hidden away are a number of interesting features. If you wander round, the village seems to take on a welcoming and hospitable atmosphere, though it is clearly unused to tourists. There are a number of pubs, and the Greyhound has a good public bar with draught lager served at a sensible price, rather than the normal inflated one.

The farm next to the motte and bailey has an early Tudor wing with timber framing and the upper storey jutting out. Near the church, and next to the Whitmoor Arms, is a sixteenth-century thatched cottage. Next to the church is a redbrick Georgian house, formerly an inn but now a shop. The church has a Norman south doorway, thirteenth-century north aisle, and fourteenth-century timber, but was largely destroyed by fire in 1926, and has been heavily restored. It has some rather ornate windows in the south chapel, and some interesting reliefs in the nave, but the overall atmosphere is one of gloom, and it has an unloved air about it.

Outside, the road is cheerful with a row of timbered shops looking very attractive. Further on, at the corner of Pound Lane, at what looks like a traffic island, is the village green. On this is the remains of the village pound, and next to it, the village lock-up, or cage. This is about 4 metres by 3 metres and made of strong blackened wooden timbers, with a tiled roof, a strong door, and a large lock. It was last used in 1848, and was re-erected in 1938. Orsett has a good bus service to Tilbury, except on Sunday, and to Grays, so it is a pleasing place to linger in, and to depart from.

The path from Orsett, behind the allotments, is hard to follow. If you carry on in a straight line from Pound Lane to the A13, do not follow the path marked on the map to Heath Place. The farmer has done his bit for conservation by planting and preserving a small area of trees near the farm for wild life; and the path has been diverted to the route described in the text. A little later on, there is a short dog-leg in the route to take us to West Tilbury village.

This has a fine village green, with the Kings Head on one side, looking rather tatty but providing food, and on the far

Village Lock-up and Pound, Orsett
View from West Tilbury Village Pond

side the village pond, now turned into a nature reserve. From
a footpath by the side of this there is a fine view of the
marshes, pylons, and the industry on the waterfront, with the
hills of Kent beyond. West Tilbury church, a little further on,
is dull and kept locked, but its site is a very historical one
indeed, and might well be visited by thousands every year—
but is not. Bishop Cedd organized the first Christian mission
to the East Saxons in the 650s from Bradwell and Tilbury,
and the site of the Tilbury mission is probably the earthworks
below the church.

Almost a thousand years later, multitudes of Englishmen
assembled here with horses and weapons, prepared to repel
the Spanish troops and keep them from London, should the
Armada defeat Drake. On 8 August 1588, Queen Elizabeth I
addressed her troops here with a speech which included
these stirring words: 'I know I have the body of a weak and
feeble woman, but I have the heart and stomach of a
King, and of a King of England, too.' A proud time, but it
was just as well Drake did defeat the Armada, since the boom
of ships and masts put across the river at Tilbury to block the
Thames was only constructed after Drake had routed the
Armada! In some respects times don't seem to have changed
too much.

The route goes back on itself slightly, to East Tilbury.
There is a footpath on the map from the next road going just
by the station, and signposted at the beginning too. However
this goes north of the station (not as on the map) and is
difficult to follow. It is hoped that this will be corrected, but
meanwhile a diversion may be necessary along the road. It is
better to head for East Tilbury station unless you are pushed
for time, and the road walk from West Tilbury to Tilbury
Riverside is 2 miles long a dull and busy road.

Route
From West Horndon station, right past Railway Inn for 400
metres to reach footpath signposted to Bulphan, on the right,
between numbers 117 and 119 on the road. At end, ahead and
under railway. Ahead with ditch on left to Field House. Then
keep ahead with ditch now on right. At field boundary go

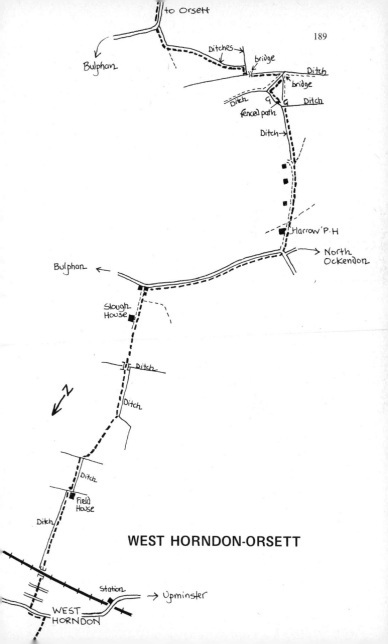

to Orsett

Bulphan

Ditches

bridge

Ditch

bridge

Ditch

Ditch

fenced path

Ditch→

Harrow P.H

→ North Ockendon

Bulphan ←

Slough House

Ditch

Ditch

N

Ditch

Ditch

Field House

Ditch

WEST HORNDON-ORSETT

Station → Upminster

WEST HORNDON

straight ahead across field following signs to rejoin ditch. Keep it on right, over footbridge and ahead with hedge and ditch on left. Join lane past Slough House and on to road.

Right along road, then left before bridge. Along track past Harrow Inn (623851) and continue along track with ditch on left past houses. Follow track until just before it turns left into farmyard, when continue with hedge and ditch on left to fenced track. The next piece is difficult to follow and heavy going under foot. Continue to where ditch crosses at right angles. Turn right and follow ditch on left for 100 metres. Cross bridge over this ditch and now follow ditch on right for 150 metres to small brick bridge, cross bridge and cross ditch immediately on left—no bridge. Right along ditch to hedge 50 metres ahead, and follow hedge and ditch left (east) to road (636843).

Right on road (S) and in 800 metres where road turns sharp left, take path to Orsett (640834). Follow road ahead, Pound Lane later Rowley Road, and later cross School Lane to go into recreation ground by right of toilets. Keep by right hedge, then to right of allotments. At end of allotments, half-left to far corner of field to meet A13 (648811), no stile. An alternative is to go straight on at end of these allotments to road and then left along the road to corner. Cross the A13, with care, and left 30 metres to stile at right of house.

The path has been diverted on this section, so follow with care. Keep to right of small spinney. Where this ends, after 200 metres, head slightly right across field (190°) to corner of field hedge opposite. Carry on in this direction (190°) for about 800 metres till get to small spinney. Through this and left by path at rear of garages to A128 road. Cross road, along Courtney Road to crossing concrete road. Turn left over stile and on path between fields to join farm road. Right on this to pass High House and footpath on left. Before Mill House, take the next path on left to Holford Road. Right to road junction (660786). Down Blue Anchor Lane to West Tilbury village green, Kings Head pub and village pond on far side of green. Retrace steps from Kings Head 100 metres back along road and right along track (iron pillar labelled 'Sir John Cass 1868') to road. Left along road for 300 metres.

Here there is both a bridleway sign, number 58, and a footpath sign. (For East Tilbury station, we should follow the footpath heading initially at 90° and going through a new housing estate, to finish just to the north of the station—not south as on O.S. maps. However, this is difficult to follow and it is easier to continue for 300 metres to road, right on road, and at bend straight on for station.) The Countryway route takes the bridleway and heads to near pylon at right of Bata shoe factory (130°) and on track in same direction to crossing-gates over railway.

Information

Distance	8½ miles; total 147 miles. Map 177.
Stations	West Horndon, East Tilbury, Tilbury Riverside: all half-hourly service to Fenchurch Street.
Buses	Eastern National 152/3/4 Chelmsford, Basildon, Grays, via Orsett: half-hourly, hourly on Sundays. 155 Orsett to Tilbury ferry: hourly, no Sunday service.
Refreshments	Harrow (623851) limited food. Greyhound (good bar) and Whitmoor Arms at Orsett, Kings Head at West Tilbury, Ship Inn at East Tilbury.
Accommodation	Bulphan motel, Gravesend, Grays, Tilbury.

This is an unusual walk, half in Essex and half in Kent, with a
ferry crossing in between. The two halves are quite different,
but each has much to offer in its own way: the Essex side with
its marshes, industry, and history, and Kent with its chalk
hills and housing.

The walk starts near East Tilbury station, and after going
over the railway we pass a large building on the left. This is
the Bata shoe factory, begun in 1932 and based on the
original Czech buildings—a model factory in its time. The
main part of East Tilbury is near the station, but a straggly
line of houses runs from there to the Thames. We pass a
worthwhile pub, the Ship, which offers food, and come to the
peculiar-looking East Tilbury church. Its peculiarity is due to
the original tower having been destroyed by the Dutch in a
naval battle in the Thames in 1667, when Admiral van
Trompe sailed up both the Thames and the Medway and
defeated the British. The church managed without a tower for
two hundred and fifty years till the Royal Engineers rebuilt it,
though only with one storey, in 1917, when they were
stationed at Tilbury fort. It is rather difficult to find the
entrance to the church, but it is open. Inside it is rather bare,
but with good stained glass above the altar, and a wall-
painting protected by glass. The north arcade still remains
from the twelfth century and there is a fish mosaic on the
floor near the vicar's stall, done in 1966.

Just past the church is Coalhouse Fort, a badly dilapidated
Victorian building, and not open to the public. The fort was
built in 1869 by General Gordon of Khartoum, who was put
in charge of rebuilding the Thames's defences after a period of
neglect. Other forts were built on the Kent side of the river at
Shornmead and Cliffe Creek, just across from Coalhouse
Fort, and at Slough Point opposite Canvey Island. These were
strongly constructed batteries with twenty or more guns in
each, and were meant to protect the military installations
along the Thames, as well as London itself. They were the
front line of defence, with the old Tilbury and Gravesend
forts relegated to the rear. The forts were never used in war,

though perhaps their presence inhibited attacks, and they have been gradually abandoned.

An earlier fort was built on this site in 1539 by Henry VIII, but nothing remains of it—apparently it was in a bad state even by 1588, the year of the Armada. Forward batteries for Tilbury fort were put here in 1795 to prepare for the French, and updated in the 1850s before the present fort was built. Nearby are the remains of old ferrymen's huts, where items of Roman pottery have been found. Some of these may be seen in the Thurrock local history museum, an excellent place.

Thurrock Council have converted the area round Coalhouse Fort to well-laid out parkland. There are boats for hire, children's amusements, beds of flowers, gorse bushes and several benches. It has not been prettified, but made into a pleasant place for relaxing and admiring the assembled mass of oil storage tanks, and watching the Thames shipping.

The path from Coalhouse Fort to Tilbury goes by the bank of the river. On the map the public path wanders away from the river occasionally, but these diversions are not easy to find and seem quite pointless. A new sea wall is being built along this stretch and this may make the going easier. At the moment the walking is on the tops of rubbish tips with broken glass galore—do not walk your dog on this! The scenery on the land side is terrible, so apart from watching where you put your feet, look at the Thames, its ships and the Kent bank. There is an interesting experience at Tilbury power station, where the route goes over a road to the jetty and under pipework by iron ladders, with the path totally enclosed by metal grilles. Not something one would wish to come across too often, but the right of way is preserved and the risk of damage minimized. It is the most unlikely path that I know of anywhere.

A little past this we come to grass again, and then pass the entrance to Tilbury Fort, the best-preserved naval fort in the country. It is open to the public, has an excellent guide-book and should not be missed.

As with Coalhouse Fort, the first proper fort was built by Henry VIII in 1539. This was repaired and extended in 1588

Tilbury Fort

after the Armada, but thereafter neglected. Plans were made by Charles II, but nothing done till after the Dutch raid of 1667 when plans were finally approved. Work was started in 1670 and was supervized by the designer Bernard de Gomme, who was Charles II's chief engineer. As is usual, construction took longer than estimated, expenditure was well over the budget and the original plan never completely finished. The building took till 1683 to complete and the water bastion, intended to protect the fort from seaward attacks, was never built. There have been later additions, with new powder magazines and accommodation for the garrison, but essentially what we see today is still Bernard de Gomme's fort.

The fort covers an area of three acres, with the moats and other redoubts outside, so there is a considerable amount to see. Despite being surrounded by the derricks of Tilbury docks on one side, and the power station chimneys on the

other, the fort still has the air of a military fort of three
hundred years ago. One can go along the walls and see the
strength of the great bastions, look at the guns, see their field
of fire, and guess the likely consequences. The batteries under
the walls, and the great powder magazines at the rear of the
parade ground can all be seen and imagined in action. The
guardhouse, with its barred windows and spy-hole in the
door, is old, but seems remarkably like a modern guardhouse.

The houses inside the fort are the officers' barracks,
originally built at the end of the eighteenth century and
renovated since. Formerly, they had a communal 'bog-house',
and it was only a later improvement that brought separate
'privies' at the bottom of each garden. And these were officers'
quarters—one can imagine the conditions of the ordinary
soldiers! Some of the houses are still occupied, and they are
not open for inspection. Outside the fort there are two moats
which could be controlled by sluices to empty them for
cleaning, or in case of frost. The most striking external feature
is the entrance, the Water Gate, designed as an impressive
monumental feature with its Ionic columns and war trophies.
The whole is a fascinating place and is my favourite stopping-
point on the entire Countryway route.

Just past the fort is the World's End pub, built in 1788, and
is where the ferryhouse was moved to in the construction of
Tilbury Fort. It provides good refreshments, and there is an
excellent view from here of Gravesend and the ferry traffic.
The ferry trip is itself interesting, and gives good views of the
great Tilbury docks, first constructed in the 1880s. The service
is a frequent one, and runs from 5.30 in the morning till 11.40
at night. There are also good train services from Tilbury
Riverside station, and, perhaps surprisingly, there is a good
café inside this large vaulted place.

Gravesend is rather a disappointment. We have been
looking at it across the river for some time, and it looked very
attractive compared with the industry of the Tilbury side. Yet
it possesses none of the historical interest nor sense of life that
Tilbury has. Tilbury is better to be in: Gravesend better to
look at. Views of Tilbury can be had from a tiny riverside
garden, reached by a hidden passageway at the side of the
New Falcon, next to the ferry. The New Falcon is rather
depressing, but does have bar billiards and Truman's ales.

Gravesend was a popular resort in the 1880s. A town guide-
book of the 1830s says, 'Go where you may, you are sure to
find shrimps for sale and lodgings to let.' Lots of steamers ran
between Gravesend and London, as it was often quicker,
before the railway, to go by boat rather than by land. Times
have changed since then, and Gravesend is now a much more
residential town, with its work found across the river. Note
the large car parks near the ferry, with the price increasing as
they get closer to it. Most of the old town has disappeared in
rebuilding, or through the numerous fires that have afflicted
Gravesend. There is no trace of Gravesend Fort, or of the old
house which General Gordon lived in. This was destroyed by
bombing in the Second World War. The parish church of St
George, near the ferry, is still here; it is a fine Georgian
church, built in 1732—replacing the earlier one destroyed by
fire in 1727! The church, after many interior alterations, is
uncluttered and spacious, after the style of a Methodist hall,
but is attractive.

In the graveyard, now laid out as a memorial garden, is a

Tilbury–Gravesend Ferry

statue and memorial to Princess Pocahontas (1595–1617).
Pocahontas was a Red Indian chief's daughter, who saved the
life of the captain of the first English settlement in North
America in Jamestown, Virginia, in 1607. Later she was taken
as part-hostage, part-guest, into the colony, and there she
married John Rolfe. They sailed to England with their son,
and Pocahontas became famous as the first Red Indian
Christian, and attended the Court. Unfortunately she became
ill, probably from tuberculosis, and died on her way back to
America. Her body was landed at Gravesend, and she was
buried in the chancel of the church, although the exact spot is
not known. The memorial statue was presented by the
Governor of Virginia in 1968.

From Gravesend, the next 9 miles of the route follows that
of another long-distance path, the Wealdway. This is about 80
miles long, and runs from the Thames at Gravesend to the
Channel, and has been worked out by a group of Ramblers
Association members. There is an initial 2 miles of road which
cannot be avoided, but this can be bussed without loss. At the
A2 crossing there is a motel which might prove useful. The
way is then by a good path to Nash Street, and near Nurstead
Court. This is the home of the Edmeades family, and parts
date back to the fourteenth century, as does the nearby
church. Nurstead itself is a village which was wiped out in the
Black Death. The route goes on from here to the station at
Sole Street where refreshments can be had at the Railway Inn.
There is a sixteenth-century timber-framed Tudor yeoman's
house nearby; it is first on the left past Manor Road, but can
hardly be seen through a forest of apple trees. It is owned by
the National Trust and the main hall is open, but only by
prior written application to the occupier.

A little off the route is the village of Cobham. Cobham
church is very large for a village church, with an enormous
chancel, built in 1220, the size of other churches' naves. The
nave was enlarged and the tower built about one hundred
years later. It has a splendid table-tomb dated 1558, some
magnificent stained glass windows and, the special feature of
the church, its collection of brasses. There are two whole rows

Leather Bottle at Cobham (Kent)

of these, all of the Cobham family, from 1320 to 1500. Just
outside the churchyard is a thirteenth-century stone house,
and one of the shops in the main street is a timber-framed
fifteenth-century cottage, now a shop.

Opposite the church is the Leather Bottle Inn, a picturesque
fifteenth-century inn, featured in *The Pickwick Papers*, and
very popular indeed. Food is served, but the crush may be too
great for comfort. If so, there are other pubs in the village
which will meet your needs in a more peaceful way. At the
end of the village is Owletts, a Charles II house, with a grand
staircase and ceiling. It is owned by the National Trust, and is
open on Wednesday and Thursday afternoons.

If you wish to see all of these, it might be better to go
directly there by path from near Ifield Court, south of
Gravesend, and on to Sole Street by a different path. It is one
of those cases where an alternative to the main route is
perhaps better than the original. In fact, I hope walkers will

not stick rigidly to the Countryway, but will use other paths where they feel so inclined and make a whole family of routes. This way, more paths will become used and less paths over-used.

Route

From East Tilbury station there ought to be a path leading to the road at 668784, but it is easier to go left out of station, left on lane, and then road for about 1,000 metres, and then left again for 400 metres to start of route proper, where there are two path signposts. Head left across field to near pylon to right of Bata factory (130°), continue on path in same direction till crossing gates over railways to road and left to reach road junction (679776). Take road signposted to East Tilbury, pass the Ship and keep on to Coalhouse Fort. Through car park at fort, toilets and water ahead, keeping to left of ditch and shortly reach sea wall. Right, west, along Thames keeping to riverside. Go over rubbish tip, unsafe for animals with its broken glass. Pass Tilbury power station on the right, over pipe work by means of iron bridge and, on the other side by sea wall, later over it by steps. Continue on round small inlet, over stile on left and carry on by Thames. At the end when Tilbury Fort is on right, go to right of embankment and passing Tilbury Fort, reach World's End pub. Keep on to Tilbury ferry and cross Thames by it.

On Gravesend side, left out of ferry terminal, along West Street. After 90 metres right up High Street. At traffic lights, cross and ahead along A227 for $1\frac{1}{2}$ miles (keep to A227) to A2 at Tollgate. Under A2 then left up to Motel. Ahead along A2, footpath past Motel on right, and right over stile at end of buildings. Along hedge on left for 30 metres, where left through gate. Half-right across field (160°)—signed to Ifield—to right edge of trees. Right along concrete track, and right at end at T-junction, then left after 10 metres along track (647700). (If you wish to see Cobham, keep straight on rather than turning left.) When hedge on left ends, go right along track for 150 metres, then left for 600 metres to road at Nash Street.

Footpath by Tilbury Power Station

Left along road, soon becoming a track, for 300 metres, then left over stile at track-bend near a field gate and down a narrow path between hedges. At end, over stile and ahead along left edge of field to far corner, where over stile and across road (648683). Ahead along left edge of field opposite, keeping to left of field till at far left corner, up track for 10 metres to Whitepost Lane, where right for 50 metres, then left down path. Left at fork 25 metres in, and 200 metres on, at road bend, go ahead along Manor Road. Right at T-junction and over railway bridge, Sole Street station and Railway Inn on right.

Information

Distance	11 miles; total 158 miles. Map 177.
Stations	East Tilbury, Tilbury Riverside: half-hourly to Fenchurch Street. Gravesend: three an hour to Charing Cross. Sole Street: hourly to Victoria.
Ferry	Gravesend to Tilbury: about every thirty minutes, 6 a.m.–10.20 p.m.
Buses	Maidstone and district 315, 316 and 322 to Tollgate on A2 from Gravesend, two an hour on weekdays and one an hour on Sunday.
Admission	Tilbury Fort, open 9.30 a.m. weekdays, 2 p.m. Sunday. Closes 4 p.m. November–February, 5.30 p.m. March, April, and October, 7 p.m. May–September. Owletts, Cobham, April–October, Wednesday and Thursday 2 p.m.–5 p.m. Tudor Yeoman's House, Sole Street. Only on written application to occupier.

Refreshments   Ship, East Tilbury. World's End, Tilbury.
Station café, Tilbury Riverside. Numerous
pubs and cafés in Gravesend. Leather
Bottle and other pubs at Cobham. Railway
Inn at Sole Street.

Accommodation   Rochester, Maidstone, Gravesend.
Kemsing Youth Hostel, via Swanley.

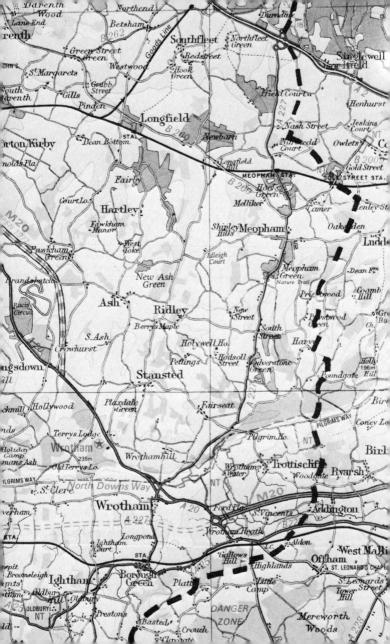

This stage leaves the Thames's influence behind and we start on the North Kent Downs. These are much less well known than the main ridge of the North Downs and have some beautiful paths. The area is remarkably well wooded and we can be very much on our own, despite being near a busy main road. In the second half of the walk we leave the hills and go through part of the 'Garden of England' with its orchards.

The route starts from Sole Street and leads across to the Cock public house. For an extra 800 metres of walking, a diversion can be made from here by a path to Luddesdowne church, and Luddesdowne Court. The church is mostly thirteenth century and has a nave and chancel extensively decorated with frescoes. Next to the church is Luddesdowne Court, one of the oldest continuously inhabited houses in the country. The great hall has an eleventh-century fireplace, an old pigeon loft, a bear pit, and some very thick flint walls. It is not open to the public. You may return from here by another path to rejoin the route before Brimstone Wood.

The section from here, or from Oakenden Road just before, to Harvel is delightful; it goes along the side of hills and through different stretches of woodland, with views of remote fields and hardly a house in sight. One might be far away from all towns in this scene. However, the absence of landmarks makes it rather easy to get lost, so be careful. Harvel is about 200 metres off route, and has a fair-sized village green with a pond. There is an old oast house turned into a private house at the corner, and just beyond is the Amazon and Tiger pub. This is very good indeed, a real village pub with many photos on the wall of the local cricket team. It is a free house, serves some snacks (not Sundays), and Fremlins bitter. The quality of its ale and its small size can make it rather crowded, but it is very companionable.

After Harvel we go by good farm tracks to Poundgate farm, and then through a large wood, Whitehorse Wood. Parts were being cleared at the time of writing, and the path was rather difficult to find across these areas. However, if you just head south to the edge of the scarp, you won't go far wrong. There are some fine views across the Weald from the top, and then an exhilarating descent across scrub to the Pilgrims' Way at the bottom.

The Pilgrims' Way is a very old track, in use before the Romans, going across the country on high and clear ground from Cornwall's tin mines and Salisbury Plain to the narrow Channel-crossing to France. It was used continuously as it was on the chalk, uncultivated and free from dense forests. Later, after the murder of Thomas à Becket, the road was used by pilgrims to Canterbury, and the name has stuck. The exact route is not certain, nor would travellers follow the same way all the time, irrespective of season, but the general way is clear. A long-distance footpath, The North Downs Way, has been opened by the Countryside Commission, which follows much of the Pilgrims' Way from Farnham (Surrey) to Dover. Most of this was already a public path, but some new rights of way have been created. We cross this route here and take a different way across Kent, but meet it again in about 30 miles.

About 500 metres past the Pilgrims' Way, we come to the Coldrum Stones. These are the remaining stones round a Neolithic burial chamber of about 2500 B.C., and is one of a little group found in this area of Kent. The barrow mound has almost disappeared, most of the stones fallen flat, and those on the edge facing the path have slipped down the slope. This has left the burial chamber open to the sky at the edge of the drop. The site was thoroughly explored in 1910 and the bones of at least twenty-two people discovered—men, women and children, thought to have been from one family. Some of the bone-remains can be seen in a glass case inside Trottiscliffe church, nearby.

Trottiscliffe, pronounced 'Trosley', church is small, and in one block, not divided into nave and chancel. It was built about 1100 using material, including sarsen stones, from the earlier churches, and on the land granted to the Bishop of Rochester in 789 by Offa, King of Mercia. The church tower was built around 1200, the north and south windows in 1350,

Amazon and Tiger at Harvel
Coldrum Stones

and other alterations have been carried out since. The church is quite plain inside with white-washed walls and old-fashioned pews.

After a large pine wood, and the first of many Kent orchards, we pass near another burial chamber into the village of Addington. This has the Angel pub and a church (kept locked), notable for its medieval brasses. In the churchyard is a curious Cleopatra-type needle of about 1800. Behind the church, we go across a newish golf course made from the old Addington Park, still with some fine trees.

There are some more orchards after this, very pleasant to walk through in spring with the blossom, and in autumn with the fallen fruit to eat. They are not the easiest of terrains, however, to follow routes through. The trees are planted in straight lines and these are almost never in the line of intended travel. One can either follow farm tracks round, trying to come out in the right place, or do a series of tacking movements through the trees. The section before Wrotham golf course is particularly tricky, with one or two hard-to-find exits, and one obstruction difficult to evade.

After a path across Wrotham golf course, we come to a road. About 500 metres from here is Great Comp, where the gardens are open some afternoons in late summer. From the road we have an interesting path through a rhododendron jungle to come out at the village of Platt. This has some old and attractive-looking stone houses near the church (locked), and a little on the right is the Blue Anchor pub, where ramblers are welcome. The village has some more attractive and expensive-looking houses on the road before our path, and then a road to Borough Green. This is a workmanlike place on the main road, with café and pubs plus a good train service. If you are youth hostelling, you can take the train one stop to Kemsing and then walk to the hostel. This is a fine old building, but the strong insistence on 'rules' at this hostel takes away some of the pleasure. However, you can wander round the village with its attractive houses, stone walls and views from the downs, and see St Edith's wishing-well on the little village green.

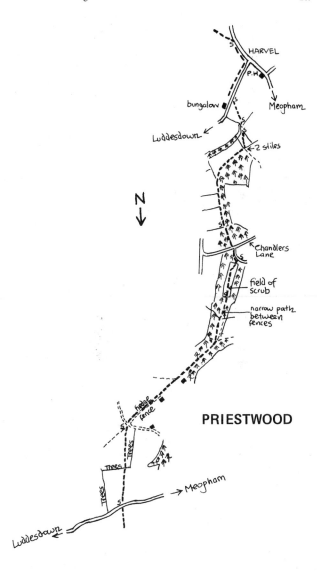

HARVEL

P.H

→ Meopham

bungalow

Luddesdown ←

← 2 stiles

N
↓

Chandlers
Lane

field of
scrub

narrow path
between
fences

hedge
fence

PRIESTWOOD

Trees

Trees

Trees

→ Meopham

Luddesdown ←

Route

From Sole Street station, across road and over stile signed to
Little Buckland, with railway line on left. At path end,
quarter-left (105°) across field. At far side, after 800 metres,
over stile and along left end of wood. Right along road and
100 metres after the Cock, right up track opposite hedge
between two fields on left. Keep ahead, soon between fields,
then along right edge of field, and enter wood. After 50 metres
right at cross tracks (260°), then after 12 metres left along
narrow winding path. After 60 metres, fork left ahead and on
to bolted gate at field corner. Through gate and ahead down
right edge of field. Climb over low rough fence, to stile and
lane at bottom (Oakenden Road).

   Cross lane, over stile into and across field (200°). Ahead
through line of trees, and ahead again to top of hill to white
gate, 30 metres right of left end of trees on summit. Over stile
and ahead up track opposite. 600 metres after third house on
right, where path splits into three, fork left downhill. Later
ahead between fences and into field of scrub. Ahead up to far
right corner. Over stile and after 12 metres, left down stony
path at path sign. At bottom cross lane, Chandlers Lane, and
ahead on path through wood. At far side, over stile and
follow right edge of field. Through trees and keep to right
edge. Bear right to keep wood on right. On reaching two
adjacent stiles, go left over left stile and uphill slightly away
from left wire fence to stile just inside trees. Over stile and
keep fence on left to second stile to enter field at corner. Head
to bungalow opposite (150°) to stile at road. Right on road to
T-junction at Harvel, pub on right (652632).

   Left along road for 200 metres, then left at stile by gate and
keep to right hedge in succession of small fields, and over
stiles until last one, where 100 metres across field in the same
direction to stile at road. Left along road for 100 metres, then
right on bend along track for 100 metres to stile, then right
again and keep by right hedge. Over stile, and then by right
hedge through second field to stile and road to Poundgate
Farm.

   Right 80 metres, and then left by clear path into woods.

Oast House nr Harvel

Continue on this path for 800 metres ignoring crossing paths until after woodland clearing. Narrow path continues ahead going slightly downhill then bending right to go along slope of hill, on path through scrub, with good views of the Weald. The path comes out down a steep bank to the left of house, to the Pilgrims' Way (653613). Right for 40 metres, then left on path with National Trust sign to Coldrum Barrow, between fence and hedge. Just past farm lane on left pass Coldrum Stones on right. Continue on track and when it bends right, take left turn. Continue on path through wood on right path. This goes into wood. At cross track, right a few metres and then left on path with pine plantations on right. Keep on this path till come out of wood by stile. Continue by left edge of field, with wood on left, until stile into orchard. Continue in same direction by edge of orchard to road at T-junction. Turn left along road signposted to Addington and continue on road over M20 into Addington.

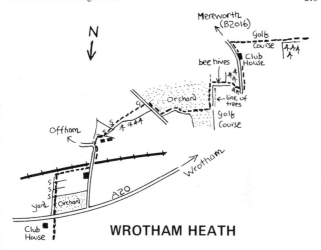

WROTHAM HEATH

Right at first right turn, Park Road, and left after 60 metres on tarmac road to St Margaret's church. Just before church, right on grass, with wall on right, across lane and into sports field. Keep by left fence to exit by a little stone bridge and short path to golf course. Ahead on track uphill, with club house on left, to road at path sign. Cross and over small stile into the edge of an orchard. Keep fence on left until stile at edge of wood, over and, keeping on bottom of slope, head across field at the bottom of little paddocks, over set of tall stiles, then right on path by railway line to road. Left on road and in 200 metres at bend right at path sign to Comp. On path to left of house to stiles, and diagonally across next field, then half-right to gate and road.

Right 70 metres, left at stile and new gate; and go by right edge of orchard. Continue with hedge on right for 400 metres till hedge bends right. Here, theoretically continue in same direction, diagonally across orchard, but it is better to follow hedge right and where this ends, follow left on clear track to the line of poplars ahead, which marks boundary of golf

Orchard Path (Kent)
Footpath with Beehives (Kent)

course. Left along this line till end of golf course. Here right on overgrown track to road 150 metres away, with a bend to the right before the end. This portion is rather difficult and has beehives on the path, which you may not wish to pass. You can avoid these hives by cutting just inside the golf course.

(You may avoid all this by continuing on the road rather than entering the orchard, sharp left *before* railway line—not as on old maps—till B2016, then left along here to rejoin original route.)

Left on road uphill and 200 metres past golf clubhouse, just past iron gate left, and opposite a stone bridleway sign on left, head right on signposted path to Platt. Slightly right across golf course (290°), heading to right of small line of poplar trees pointing away from you, and left of inset line of bushes. Head towards path ahead, to right of trees and then on field with wood on right to come on to road by the side of a house, Valley Wood. Cross and take enclosed path by left of drive. At end of fence, straight ahead over cross tracks, then fork right 20 metres on. Continue on path through rhododendrons, ignoring side paths until come to church at Platt, pub on right. Left and through car park and right down to road, then cross over and take furthest fork, signed to Plaxtol. After 300 metres, opposite start of pavement, right on track before old oast house. Keep hedge on left, and in 800 metres reach road. Right on road. To continue walk: in 200 metres left on to farm track. For station: continue on road for 800 metres to A25, left and then right into station.

Information

Distance	10 miles; total 168 miles. Maps 177 and 188.
Stations	Sole Street: hourly to Victoria. Borough Green: two an hour to Victoria.
Buses	Maidstone and District 322 Gravesend, Meopham, Borough Green. Hourly.

Admission   Great Comp, Wednesdays and Sundays, 15
                   May–15 October, 2–6 p.m.

Refreshments   Amazon and Tiger at Harvel, Angel at
                   Addington, Blue Anchor at Platt. Several
                   pubs and cafés on A25 at Wrotham.

Accommodation Kemsing Youth Hostel, Ryarsh, West
                   Malling, Maidstone, Wrotham.

This stage is my choice for the most beautiful of the whole route. We start by going through a number of orchards and gradually gain height so that we begin to get views of the surrounding country. Then, after the parkland of Fairlawne and the Tudor Ightham Mote, we keep to the main sandstone ridge for the rest of the walk. The path sticks to the edge where the woods on the top meet the farming land of the Wealden clay. It gives superb views of the Weald, which change as the path goes at different heights along the route. The walk is splendid at all times of the year, but best of all is walking it on a fine winter's day, making a path through the clean snow and having the exhilaration of seeing the whole plain below. One really enjoys eating in the evening and sitting in front of a good fire after a walk like this. Such days can be relived in the memory for years after.

The first part of the walk has an attractive downhill path to Basted where there are some offices hidden away and fitting in quite well with the rural scene. The Plough is nearby, too. After a pleasant walk by a stream, the path takes an interesting little route across fields and orchard to come to a very out-of-place used-car lot! Down the road from here is the village of Plaxtol—rather posh but with three pubs and a restaurant. It also has a church opened in 1649 during the Commonwealth, and hence with no dedication. The next stretch presents a problem, as the true line of the right of way was accidentally planted over by an impenetrable set of trees. Our route follows the practice of local riders and goes round the obstacle, which in this case is probably a satisfactory solution. It is not a good general policy, though, as it then becomes difficult to follow routes from maps or for new owners to know the true position.

After the next road there is a short section of path rather too well-used by horses, but we can escape this by going over a stile and across the cropped grassland, delightful to walk on, of Fairlawne Park. Fairlawne House, opposite, used to be the home of Sir Henry Vane who was executed by Charles II for his support of Oliver Cromwell. Vane used his trial to make a

spirited defence of the sovereignty of Parliament. A short
distance past the park we go along the drive of Ightham
Mote. This is a beautiful old manor house built with stone as
mellow as can be, with timber framing above, and surrounded
by a moat filled with clear, fresh water. There is a little bridge
leading across the moat, which has ducks and swans to make
the scene perfect. The gardens are formally laid out and you
may see peacocks wandering through. The house was built in
1340 with external additions in 1520, but little altered since
then. The great hall (1340) has its original oak ceiling, and
the entrance tower (1480) its original wooden doors.
Unfortunately, the house is privately owned and only open to
the public on Friday afternoons, so there is little opportunity
to see inside. However, excellent close-up views of the exterior
can be had from the drive which is a public right of way and
which our route goes along.

The next stretch of the route to Knole Park is the scenic
highlight of the walk. We stick rather at the bottom of the
slope of the hills and go on a good path by the edge of the
trees. There are other paths, though, so it is not difficult to go
astray. Despite its beauty and views, the walk is relatively
little used and you can often be quite alone on it—though
perhaps not so much after this book is published. There is no
refreshment available on the line of the route, but there is a
small pub, the White Rock, 800 metres off the way at Under
River. It is not tarted up and has original oak beams, but does
not serve food.

Our route goes through only the edge of Knole Park, but if
you have any spare time it is worth walking through this
splendid deer park to the house. The park is open to the
public every day by permission of the owner, Lord Sackville,
and provides an excellent route to Sevenoaks if you wish to
finish there. Knole House, one of the largest private houses in
England, is now owned by the National Trust, and is open,
except in the depth of winter, on Wednesdays to Saturdays,
and on Sundays from August to November.

The first impression the house makes is one of size. It is a
great jumbled mass of buildings, roofs, chimneys, and

View of Fairlawne
Ightham Mote

gables—looking more like a fortified town than a house for a single family. The house covers four acres and has seven courtyards, and is supposed to have fifty-two staircases, and 365 rooms!

Buildings existed in at least 1370, and probably earlier, but it was transformed into a great house by Bourchier, Archbishop of Canterbury, who bought it in 1456 for £266 13s. 4d. The price may have been low as the previous owner's father, Lord Saye, the Lord Treasurer, together with his son-in-law, the Sheriff of Kent, were beheaded by Jack Cade in the Peasants' Revolt of 1450. Two weeks earlier Cade's rebels had ambushed the royal troops on the edge of Knole Park, and defeated them.

Several archbishops followed Bourchier until Henry VIII confiscated the house from Archbishop Cranmer in 1538. After a period of confusion, the present family, the Sackvilles, gained uncontested possession in 1603, and have remained at Knole ever since.

Entering the house by the main gate we pass through the Green Court to the Stone Court, a large courtyard paved with stones over reservoirs of water for the house. The attention to detail in the house is shown by the leaden drainpipes, dated 1605, which are all different. The Great Hall, covered with ornate wooden panelling and carving, is where the family would eat, with an orchestra in the musicians' gallery. The house is filled with the family's furniture, tapestries, pictures, silver and rugs. A special feature is the original upholstery and coverings on the chairs and sofas—they are rather faded and tatty but still lasting after three or four hundred years' use. There is good oak everywhere, but, paradoxically for modern tastes, it is painted a rather dingy cream which hides the wood's texture. The Ballroom is an immense room with magnificent oak panelling with carvings of mermaids and grotesque figures, and a plasterwork ceiling decorated with flowers and acorns. The Venetian Ambassador's bedroom has a huge and sumptuous four-poster bed; the crimson drawing-room has several Reynolds; and the Cartoon Gallery has

Knole House (220–1)
Goathurst Common, nr Sevenaoks

copies of Raphael cartoons on its red velvet-covered walls. There is an air of luxury everywhere but somehow, despite this and the size of the house, it still seems lived in and a home.

After the splendours of Knole Park, we go on a little-used path to Sevenoaks Weald, where the Windmill pub is 400 metres off the way. The next part of the route has less spectacular views, but it is still pleasant and we pass one or two attractive farms, particularly Wickhurst Manor. We reach high ground again just before Ide Hill, and have good views behind us over the large new Bough Beech reservoir. This adds another touch of interest but its size makes it look out of place. There are some really splendid old beeches here, with a wide carpet of grass to set them off. It is a perfect place for a picnic with children.

On the road just before the village is the Wheatsheaf, a favourite place with ramblers. It serves food, has a large garden

and good views. Ide Hill, itself, just beyond, is an attractive little village with a large green, shops and two pubs: the Cock, with food, and the Crown which has hot food as well as snacks. This stage finishes at Ide Hill, but transport is not as good as it might be from here, with a bus only every two hours and none on Sundays. In summer one can continue the route to Chartwell and catch a bus from there, but otherwise the alternative is to walk to Sundridge on the A25 for a bus to Sevenoaks, or Bromley and London. Youth hostellers should press on to Crockham Hill.

Route
From Borough Green over railway bridge, left to main road, left along this and first right past pub. After 800 metres, right down farm track by a concrete milk-stand.

Ahead and at fork, left (ahead) and go left of wood. Along

Brambly footpath nr Basted

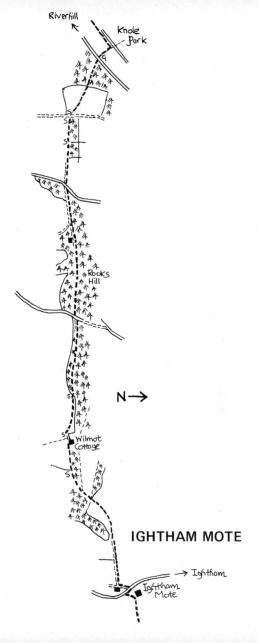

Riverhill

Knole Park

Rocks Hill

N→

Wilmot Cottage

IGHTHAM MOTE

→ Ightham

Ightham Mote

attractive path and to road at site offices, Butterworth's. Left at road, and right along track just before bridge. The Plough is up hill—100 metres on right. Ahead along track with stream on left to road. Right up road for 100 metres, then into orchard at top of hill. Straight ahead away from road on track (190°) under pylons and over stile at far side. Across small stream by stepping stones and over another stile. On up into field and follow right edge to farm lane by right of old-car lot. Ahead up track to road. Right along road for 100 metres, then left along track passing Grove Cottage on right.130 metres up track, go left through hedge and right on track with hedge on right. After 200 metres follow track as it bends left (this is not quite the right of way but it is used, as the true way is planted over by trees). When track comes in from left, go sharp right up through belt of trees to fields. Straight ahead across narrow belt of field (240°) to go along left edge of wood. At far corner slightly right (260°) to left end of belt of trees ahead, then right along edge of field with trees on left. At field corner, ahead, over stile by gate and along track (ignore track forking right 20 metres in). Later over stile and on to road at junction (591540).

Cross and left down bridleway. At bottom after 700 metres, through gate and follow bridlepath with hedge on right to T-junction. Here, right over stile and ahead between hedgerows (290°). At fork, follow fence on left and through Ightham Mote. Right at road, then left after 35 metres through farm buildings. After 80 metres, in front of oast houses, right on sunken track going into fields (280°). Ahead on track, ignoring bridlepath on right later, but keep ahead following footpath. Later path goes down through strip of woodland, then with wood on right, over stile and on up track. Past house on right, Wilmot Cottage, on through kissing gate, and over stile into field. Right up bank and along edge of field. After 100 metres, over stile on right, then left along path just inside wood.

After 700 metres reach lane and turn left (566530) for 15 metres, then right up path, running into track, in 400 metres by house. Track later becomes lane. At junction, cross half-

Deer at Knole Park

right to Shepherds Mead. Left along drive for 10 metres, then right along path between fences. At second stile, over crossing track and ahead over another stile into field. Diagonally (305°) across field to far left corner. Over stile, across path and ahead to road. Cross through gate into Knole Park (549531). (Sevenoaks station ahead across park in 2 miles.)

Ahead 100 metres to tarmac lane. Left along it for 1,200 metres and then left on lane to gate in fence and road. Right along road.

Cut down on path left when in sight of major road, A225, then left along road. After 200 metres, round long right-hand bend, cross (beware: dangerous) and right (320°) down path opposite house, with fence on left and wood on right. Ahead for 1,200 metres until path comes in from right then after 80 metres, hard left down track into field. Follow right edge and through gate. Diagonally left down next field to gate, then on

through tunnel (533517) under A21. Follow track, through farmyard, and right out of it. After 70 metres, half-left (240°) across field towards church. Over stile at far side, and on to road (528513). Right till a few metres past road junction, left over stile by bus stop space. Follow hedge on left to bottom, over stile and half-right (270°) up towards farm, the right house of two, over gate and through farmyard, right and left. Half-right over field (280°) to gate in line of trees. Through and across next field to bar stile. Over, through trees, over metal-rail stile and across (260°) down to stream by gap in hedge, to join wire mesh fence on left, then in same direction at corner ahead (275°) to gap in hedge with gate just beyond. Through gate and on down to gate and lane (518512).

Left, then right, to Wickhurst Manor Farm. Over stile at end, by white gate, and ahead across field (290°) towards house on hill. At field corner right uphill with hedge on right. Through gate at top then left along lane. After 80 metres, right over stile before Hatchlands Farm. Along left hedge and left over stile and footbridge, then right by left edge of wood (320°) along track. At end, over stile and ahead across two fields (300°) and into wood by stile 200 metres from its right end. Out of wood over stile and half-right (300°) uphill. At top of rise, over stile in barbed-wire fence and continue to left end of trees, and stile. Over and ahead along right edge of field for 120 metres. Over stile in corner, then along narrow path just inside wood. In 200 metres this swings right up hill. At top, left along path parallel to road on right, later crossing lane (496518) that goes left downhill.

Ahead for 800 metres, then fork left uphill. Then left 100 metres on at cross tracks (230°). Descend with fir plantations on left and right, then ahead for 400 metres to driveway turning circle. Right and take the lower, left, of two tracks. Later lane comes in from left just before main road with Wheatsheaf on right (489516).

Left along B2042, then right in 100 metres to Ide Hill. You may catch an occasional bus from here to Sevenoaks or walk up the road to Sundridge. Youth hostellers should continue on the route to Crockham Hill.

IDE HILL (a)

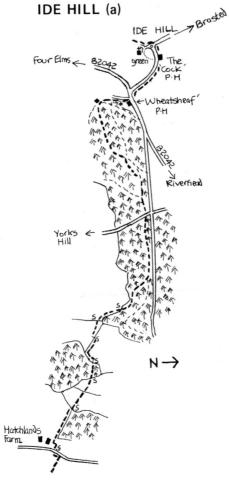

Information

Distance	10½ miles; total 178½ miles. Map 188.
Stations	Borough Green: half-hourly to Victoria. Sevenoaks: four an hour to Charing Cross and Waterloo.
Buses	Ide Hill to Sevenoaks, London Country 404 about three-hourly, no Sunday service. London Country 483 Sevenoaks to Westerham. 454 Sevenoaks to River Hill, Tonbridge hourly, no Sundays. Maidstone and District 322 Borough Green to Plaxton hourly, two-hourly Sundays.
Admission	Ightham Mote, Fridays only, 2–5 p.m. Knole House, April–September, Wednesday–Saturday 10 a.m.–5 p.m., Sundays 2–5 p.m. March, October and November, Wednesday–Saturday 11 a.m.–4 p.m., Sunday 2–4 p.m.
Refreshments	Plough at Basted, Papermakers' Arms and Rorty Crankle at Plaxtol. The Forge restaurant at Plaxtol, White Rock pub at Under River, no food (556521). Windmill at Sevenoaks Weald. Wheatsheaf, Cock, and Crown, at Ide Hill.
Accommodation	Difficult. Crockham Hill Youth Hostel, Sevenoaks, Westerham.

This stage takes us through the wooded commons of the sandstone country on the Kent border with Surrey. It has good views at the beginning, but later pleasure comes from the variety and splendour of the trees on the way. The route goes by some of the finest property of the National Trust: Ide Hill, Toy's Hill, Crockham Hill, and, of course, Chartwell. If you have not visited Chartwell before, it is worth timing the walk to make sure you get there while it is open.

The walk starts by the church at Ide Hill and goes up to a little open space at the top of the hill. This has a steep slope in front and gives very good views over the Weald, with Bough Beech reservoir prominent. There is an intricate piece of route-finding after the view point, till we reach a good path going across a hidden valley with a stream in the middle. The woods on the other side are owned by the National Trust, and just before our final left turn out of these woods we can turn right instead to reach another National Trust property, Emmetts. The house is not open, but the four acre shrub garden is open to the public on Wednesday and Saturday afternoons in summer. Emmetts can also be reached by walking from Ide Hill 800 metres down the Sundridge road.

The area around has the general name of 'the Chart', which often appears on maps round here, and means an area of rough common land. After the Chart there is a little valley before the tiny hamlet of French Street, another uphill stretch through woods, and then a downhill path with the grounds of Chartwell to be seen on your left.

Chartwell is a pleasant, large but unpretentious country house, with gardens set in eighty acres of parkland, and was the home of Sir Winston Churchill for over forty years. This makes it one of the most visited of the National Trust's properties, so you may have rather a wait to get inside the house. Numbered tickets are given, however, and you can spend the time looking round the gardens and park. There are several levels of garden so that the stream can be used to make different types of pond: a fish pond, a swimming pool, and a lake with an island, created by Churchill. The views are

of the little valley, and of a large well-wooded area of the Weald. The pleasure that this gave must have intensified Churchill's will to keep Britain as it was, and provided comfort against the horror of Hitler. Churchill loved Chartwell; he had the extension built, but did most of the garden walls and layout himself. The studio in the garden has Churchill's easel, chair and mementoes, and about seventy of his paintings. The interest of these lies in the painter rather than the paintings, although one or two of his children are rather better.

The house itself does not have many rooms for its size, but they are all large ones and all have tables on which to read or play cards. It is full of little nooks and crannies where one can hide oneself and be away from others, and the whole is very homely.

The study is the heart of Chartwell. Churchill used it constantly for the whole of his forty years' residence, and it is where he did most of his writing. It is a big barn of a place, rough-hewn and plain with wooden floors and only a tiny carpet. The desk at which he worked is a plain stand-up desk with open shelves, given to him by his children in 1949 but similar to one he had designed himself and used over the years. The room has lots of space for books but, again, the bookshelves are big and rough, such as can be bought from second-hand shops. The study has accumulated lots of gifts and trophies over the years, but there is nothing showy about it. It remains a well-used workmanlike place. Seeing the house adds something to one's knowledge and appreciation of Churchill. The house is open (except in winter) late mornings and afternoons at week-ends, and afternoons only on Tuesdays, Wednesdays, and Thursdays. There is a restaurant here, and snacks are available too.

A bus runs in summer via Westerham to London. Westerham is a busy market town, associated with two famous men—Winston Churchill, and General Wolfe—and a statue to each stands on the green. There is a variety of shops, cafés, inns, including the George and Dragon, an old coaching

View from Ide Hill
Statue of Winston Churchill at Westerham

inn, and several fine-looking houses. Westerham church is
beautiful, with lots of stained glass, a thirteenth-century
chancel and fourteenth-century north chapel and a font where
Wolfe and Winston Churchill's grandsons were baptized. The
sanctuary lamp in the north chapel was given by Winston
Churchill. There is also rather a splendid view east from the
churchyard. Quebec House, in which Wolfe lived his early life,
is open in summer on Tuesday, Wednesday and Sunday
afternoons.

The walk from Chartwell goes up a steep path, well-used by
horses, over part of Crockham Hill Common to the road
leading to Crockham Hill village. There is a friendly youth
hostel in the village, much patronized by foreigners in
summer. If you wish to go there, walk along a little lane to
Froghole and then take an excellent little path, hidden but
signposted, going down a long flight of stone steps by the side
of gardens, to go across a field to Crockham Hill church.

Octavia Hill, the founder of the National Trust, has a monument inside the church and her grave is second to the right under the branches of a yew tree. There is also a pleasant little green, part-orchard, in the centre of the village, dedicated to her memory. It is a good place to eat sandwiches, helping yourself to an apple from the trees on the green. Octavia Hill was a devoted opener up of footpaths, so you are doing her honour in the best possible way! There are two pubs in the village, the Crown, and the Royal Oak, both of which serve food.

The original route continues across Crockham Hill Common, a birch wood with several clearings and many different paths, when you should come out at Kent Hatch Lodge on the border of Kent and Surrey. It is easy to go wrong across here, as I have done, but also easy to get back on the road to the Lodge. From here there is an interesting wide path, not following the right of way line on the map, across mixed woodland to come out at Moorhouse Bank. Down the road from here, on the main A25, is the Grasshopper Inn, a very large 'Tudor' roadhouse with restaurant and bars. The path goes on behind the cricket ground by some attractive paths across different parts of Limpsfield Common to come out at Hurst Green. The beeches are very fine early on, and the paths are satisfying to tramp in autumn. Later there are a number of paths, making it rather hard to pick out the right one, but with good views and benches to admire them from. In the middle you approach quite close to Limpsfield and, if you are keen on music, you may wish to see Delius's grave in Limpsfield churchyard. It is near an old yew tree, in the third row of graves from the road, north of the church. Hurst Green station is slightly nearer than Oxted station, but if you are looking for refreshments you would do better to go to Oxted. The main shopping centre with the usual selection of chain stores is in new Oxted near the station; the best pubs, however, are in old Oxted.

Crockham Hill Youth Hostel

Route

The route starts at Ide Hill, but it is somewhat difficult to get there by public transport. There is an occasional bus from Sevenoaks, though not Sundays; otherwise you have to catch the Westerham bus, alight at Sundridge (483553) and walk 2 miles south to Ide Hill Green (483518).

Leave the Cock on right, then half-left across green (240°) to Ide Hill National Trust sign and entrance. Along drive for 60 metres, then fork right and along path with field on right for 150 metres to viewpoint at open space. A quarter-right downhill (235°) and into trees. Path bends right and after spring and stream left and over stile. Right, and follow fence on left with wood on right. Over stile at end, then left downhill with fence on left to valley bottom and footbridge. Over and ahead with hedge on left (320°) to left corner, where over stile and in same direction (320°) with hedge on right and then straight on up to woodland. Left by side of wood and after 100 metres right over stile into wood. Ahead (300°) up path. Just beyond house on left, keep to right fork uphill. Right (50°) at top (474518) on wide track and continue on main track for 600 metres, to where it descends between banks to cross tracks then swings right uphill. Continue on

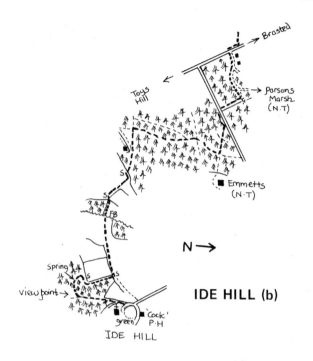

IDE HILL (b)

IDE HILL

main track till, in about 200 metres, 40 metres after hill
flattens, left at cross tracks (475524). (Right here for
Emmetts.) Ahead (290°) and reach road in 300 metres, where
left and after 70 metres right down path (335°), ignoring left
fork 5 metres in. Keep to fence on right and at metalled track
left, later joining driveway just before main road (468524).

  Right along road and after 100 metres left on narrow path
to Westerham. Later swing right with fence to stile. Over stile,
and ahead (320°) across field to stile at end of left hedge, by
sign to 'French St'. Over and down to farm track, where right
for 10 metres, then left over stile and half-left (290°) down to
stile, and footbridge. Up field with fence on left to top
(458527), where over stile and left along lane at French Street.

View from Chartwell

After 80 metres right up drive past Mannings Wood on left
and ahead along grass track. When metalled track comes in
from right, turn sharp left (140°). Ahead along wide track to
road. Cross and ahead (240°) down path, ignoring footpath
on right. After 70 metres left down path between fences
with Chartwell on left and through stile at end to road
(454518).

Across road and fork left uphill (240°). Path unclear at first,
but soon clears as it is joined by earlier muddy right path.
Keep on this bearing until shortly after the path crosses a
gravel one, when veer right at fence. 15 metres on, ahead
down the hill to B2026 (448514). (To get to Crockham Hill
Youth Hostel, left down road 200 metres, then left down
track signed to Froghole. Take right fork after 150 metres,
then after further 200 metres, when road bends left, go
straight on at footpath sign to Crockham Hill church, by right
of new double garage. Go down private-looking flight stone
steps, later with hedge on right, to stile. Continue with hedge
on right to second stile, left down field, right at bottom edge,
not over stile, to later stile into Church Lane. Up lane to road
where left for 300 metres to hostel.)

Cross half-right into April Cottage drive, and after 60
metres right into wood and immediately take centre track of
three uphill (280°). At top, in front of The Warren, slightly
right (310°) along grass path. Ahead for 800 metres over many
cross tracks to Kent Hatch Lodge (439518). There are many
tracks in this wood and when in doubt take right forks. Be
careful of path signs as there are several footpaths. At Kent
Hatch Lodge, right and in 30 metres over stile. Take left track
and after 200 metres, turn left on track to reach road in 100
metres, opposite private road to Wood End etc. (439521).
Half-right on enclosed bridleway to Limpsfield. Reach cross
tracks in 300 metres where ahead (310°) with forestry hut on
left. Follow cinder track until it bends left, then keep on with
field on right. Follow path, gradually bearing left, and in 400
metres reach stile, where over and left along gravelled drive to
road at stile (431530). Cross road to Limpsfield Common,
Moorhouse Bank (National Trust), and ahead behind cricket
pavilion. 50 metres on, downhill, then, after 40 metres, right

Ide Hill to Hurst Green

LIMPSFIELD COMMON

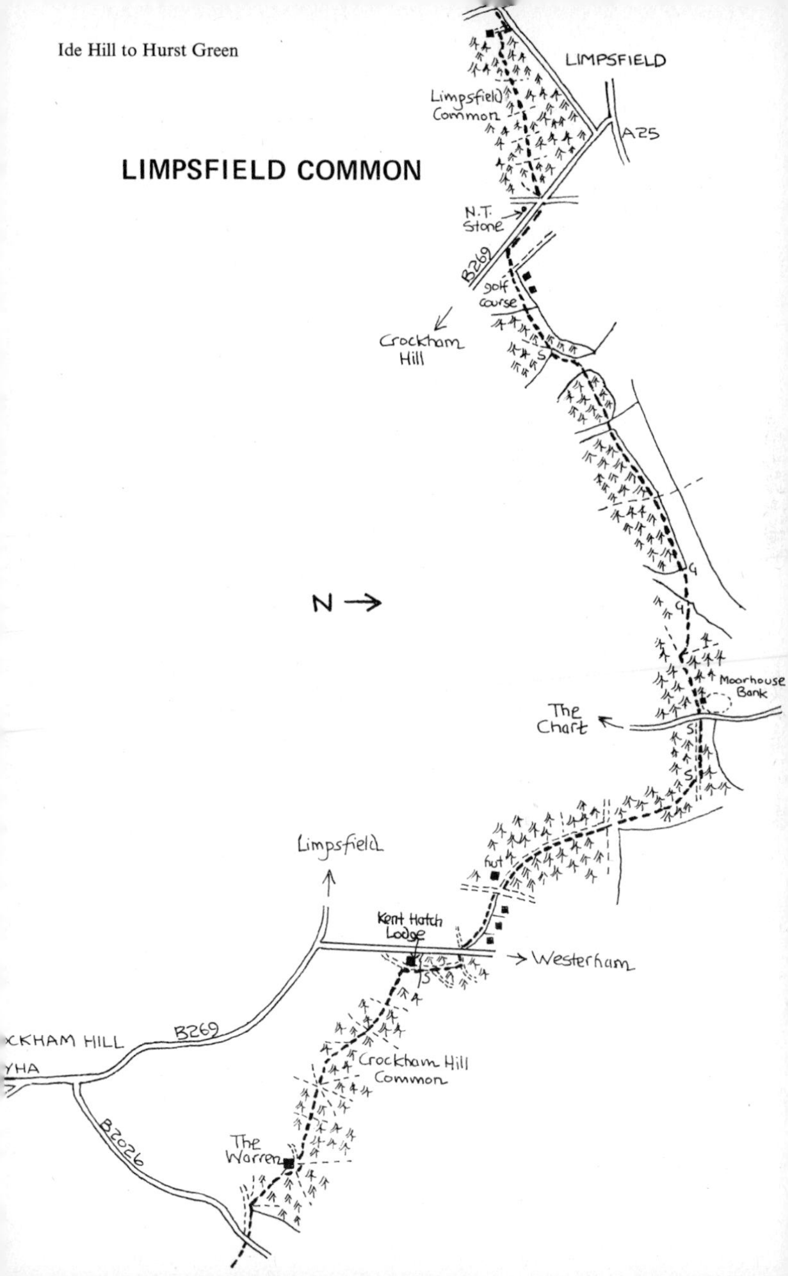

LIMPSFIELD

Limpsfield
Common

A25

N.T.
Stone

B269

golf
course

Crockham
Hill

N →

Moorhouse
Bank

The
Chart

Limpsfield

hut

Kent Hatch
Lodge

→ Westerham

CKHAM HILL

B269

YHA

Crockham Hill
Common

B2026

The Warren

by clump of tall beeches, then after 25 metres fork left to valley bottom. Here left and follow fence on right for 100 metres, then through gate and ahead (270°) across corner of field to gate in 150 metres (425529). Through into wood and ahead over cross tracks, keeping to valley bottom. Over stile, across field strip for 50 metres and into small wood. Out of wood and cross corner of field (270°) to fence, where left, with fence on right to stile in 200 metres by Titsey Estate sign. Take right-hand path by edge of wood, then with golf course on left and houses on right. At cross tracks with sunken path on left go half-right by sixteenth tee to go by rough to road (414523).

Right along road and in 200 metres cross road to National Trust commemorative stone. Over road coming in from left to Pains Hill, and take second track on right with sign 'No Horses' (270°). Continue on this path over several crossing tracks, staying in valley bottom, till, after 400 metres, path bears right then left and climbs, bearing right at valley side to join a gravel drive, Stone Vale. Continue on drive to road. Left for 100 metres to road junction (405523).

Cross road to path—sign 'No Horses'—and up hill (270°) with path gently bearing left along top of ridge, passing wooden seat on left. Then continue on path parallel to line of houses on right, past National Trust sign 'Turning point only', left (230°) and in 50 metres reach well-defined path on top of the ridge. Right on this, soon passing wooden bench, then seat. Leave common at Pope's Cottage and follow track downhill between wooden fences to road (399520). (For Hurst Green Station, left on this, Rockfield Road, then right on Wolf's Hill and Hurstlands to reach station in 1000 metres.) To continue walk, straight ahead on Icehouse Wood Road.

Information

Distance	8½ miles; total 187 miles. Maps 187 and 188.
Stations	Sevenoaks: four an hour to Charing Cross. Hurst Green: hourly to Victoria.
Buses	London Country 404 about every three hours, no Sunday service, Sevenoaks to Ide Hill. London Country 485 Crockham Hill to Westerham, every two hours, no Sunday service. Green Line 706 extends to Chartwell on Wednesday and Thursday afternoons in summer.
Admission	Emmetts garden, April and July–October, Wednesday and Saturday; May–June, Tuesday–Thursday and Sunday. All 2–6 p.m. Chartwell house and gardens, March to November, Saturday and Sunday, 11 a.m.–6 p.m. Tuesday, Wednesday, Thursday, 2–6 p.m., or sunset if earlier. Quebec House, Westerham, March, Sundays only. April–October daily except Thursdays and Saturdays, 2–6 p.m.
Refreshments	Crown and Royal Oak at Crockham Hill. Cafés and numerous pubs at Westerham. Grasshopper at Moorhouse Bank (430533). Several pubs at Old Oxted.
Accommodation	Difficult. Crockham Hill Youth Hostel, Westerham, Oxted.

There is a mixture of scenery on this stage, with the secluded
Marden valley, the track along the North Downs ridge, and
the motorways round Merstham.

Soon after the start at Hurst Green from Icehouse Wood
Road we pass through a fascinating old wooden turnstile to
get on to the footpath and pass the remains of another one on
the way. These have obviously been here for a long time, but
why is a mystery. The route then goes past an old mill pond
to come to Oxted and its High Street. The town has been
bypassed so we can see it in peace, and it makes a good
picture with a number of colour-washed cottages dating from
the fifteenth to eighteenth centuries, and separated from the
traffic by a causeway. The street is rather infested by antique
shops, but you can try and ignore their presence; look instead
at the George Inn, the seventeenth-century Crown, and the
sixteenth-century Old Bell. This last has a restaurant and
serves Truman's ales—but by some quirk of fate, I have never
tried any of these places so I can make no recommendations!

The path continues under the new bypass to the road by
Barrow Green Farm, with a stone cat on the roof. The house
is sixteenth-century, but not the cat! Opposite this is the
seventeenth-century Barrow Green Court, now protected
from public view by new tall fences, barbed wire and guard
dogs. Such care is very much out of place in this area, or any
other, and makes one wonder what secret business can be
going on that has to be protected so securely and so
hideously. The path continues up what used to be a peaceful
path, but this is no longer so with the construction of the new
M25 motorway across the route. We can try and ignore this,
and just look at the path making a clear trail through the
chalk up to the top of Tandridge Hill.

Over the hill the path becomes rather gloomy going
through an overgrown wood, but it suddenly comes out and
we see a beautiful grass valley below, the Marden valley. It is
hard to imagine we are only 15 miles from the centre of
London. It is always quiet here, and even after a
thunderstorm, with the air thick and the sound carrying for

miles, one could hear only the birds. By some miracle it has
been preserved from development, though it was intended to
run the railway line through here from the abortive Channel
tunnel. The original village of Marden was wiped out by the
Black Death in 1348. A new mansion was built here in 1677,
but it was destroyed by fire in 1879. The Victorian house
which replaced it now houses the Convent of the Sacred Heart
girls' school, and very fine it looks from the outside.

One can walk down the valley to Woldingham to catch a
train to London, but the Countryway climbs back out again
on another path with beautiful views of the valley. This used
to be very difficult to find or follow till Surrey County Council
built the fine wooden steps at the start, with a stone signpost,
and cleared the path through the woods. This has effectively
produced a valuable public amenity for a minimal cost
compared with, say, a 'leisure centre'! Walkers may be slightly
nervous of a bull sometimes seen the other side of the

footpath, but he has cows and seems to know his place. A little bit on from here I had a discussion with a farmer who claimed there was no path and that anyway no one had used it for forty years. Yet, I had used it before a number of times, sometimes with parties, and on the other side of the field in question there was a public-path sign pointing back the way we had come. Be wary if you receive local information of this kind, although this was very exceptional, and most of the farmers and other residents on the route have been pleased to see walkers.

We meet the North Downs Way again just before the A22, where there is a handy bus between Godstone and Caterham, and a Green Line to London. Our route now follows the general line of the North Downs Way for the next 18 miles or so to Hackhurst Downs. The aim of both this and the Countryway is to stick to the North Downs ridge for the views, but the two routes do not coincide everywhere because the Countryway tries to aim for variety of scenery rather than purity of line. The new footbridge built to carry the North Downs Way over the A22 is a considerable help, particularly on summer weekends, and the path takes us to Gravelly Hill, where there are seats and good views across the weald. Leith Hill can be picked out 15 miles away on the right, and, in the distance, 25 miles away, the line of the South Downs can be seen stretching across the horizon.

The route then avoids some road-walking by going through the scrub and trees by chalk paths, which can be slippery in the wet. Just off White Hill, 800 metres on, is the Harrow, a rather busy pub. This has modestly priced food, a garden with lots of seats and is used to rambling parties, in spite of being carpeted throughout. But do take care if you have muddy boots.

There is a good tramp by lanes before we cut down across fields, getting a view again, to go under the M23. Coming out of the tunnel, take a look right. Along here is where the terminus of the old Surrey iron railway used to be, at Merstham quarries. This was the first public railway in the world, constructed from Wandsworth to Croydon in 1803 and

Old Bell at Oxted

extended to Merstham in 1805. It was horse-drawn, and the horse or mule walked between the 1.37 metres (4 feet 6 inches) tracks. The line closed in 1838, but a short length of track has been reconstructed and can be seen outside the Joliffe Arms, Merstham (at the junction of the B2031 to Alderstead Farm and the A23).

Other forms of transport now concern us, as after a short stretch we go on a bridge over a second motorway, the M25. If you look back at this bridge you will see it is delicately curved and, unlikely as it might seem, is a beautiful piece of architecture. There are also good views from the bridge—not quite so good as of the bridge itself but still worth looking at. There are five motorway bridges in less than 800 metres; one for a road, two for the railway, and two for footpaths. If we are to have more motorways, this section is a model to be repeated elsewhere.

We have yet more bridges, this time over the railway—and not qualifying for any design awards—to come out in Merstham station. The stage could not end more conveniently! Just out of the station yard is the nondescript Feathers Inn. Step inside for a surprise: it has old brown wood, bubble glass, mirrors, red chairs and hidden alcoves, giving it an authentic Edwardian look. It serves snacks and salads in the bar, there is a separate steak bar, and a good beer garden; and this very tatty-looking author was made most welcome. Over the road is Quality Street, a survival from old Merstham, with some attractive eighteenth-century houses. The Old Forge is fifteenth-century, and Merstham church, reached by one of the motorway bridges, is twelfth-century. It has a thirteenth-century tower and brasses from 1420–1580, but because the church is kept locked, all that you may be able to see is an eighteenth-century sundial over the south door. Merstham is a surprising place—have a look round while you are here.

Cleared footpath at Woldingham

Route

From Hurst Green station, left along Hurstlands, Wolf's Hill then left by Rockfield Road until Icehouse Wood Road. Left on here and after 700 metres, opposite Icewood House, right along drive to Three Hedges, after 50 metres, ahead through old wooden turnstile and on path. Left at road and after 10 metres, right down Spring Lane. Continue till after mill pond (389518), right on path. At end, left up Springfield Road and right at top to Oxted.

Cross High Street, Old Bell on right, down Sandy Lane and under A25. 200 metres on at the Lodge, where road heads right (383524), left on footpath over stile and follow left edge of two fields. Through small iron gate and cross road into lane. Ahead, lane becoming a track, on footbridge over M25 then left on path and take a bridlepath by edge of small wood. Climb to top and cross road (369536). Cross road between two posts on path. After 60 metres right on broad track (10°)

A22 - GRAVELLY HILL

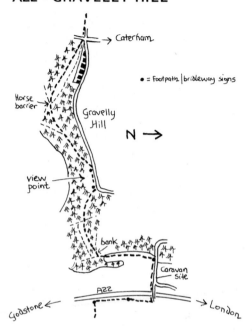

which goes along the top of the ridge, gradually bearing left, and passing deep hollow on right with the remains of an adventure area, to stile. Over stile and downhill with wood on right to second stile. Left down metalled track to reach convent drive in 50 metres, right along this. Pass tennis courts on left, then 10 metres after fence on left ends, go up steps by stone footpath sign (360547). Left along terraced track into wood and over stile. Follow winding path. Barbed-wire fences gradually close in to lead over two stiles and into field. Follow fence on right for 50 metres till just before electric cable. Then left across field, following a short line of trees, and then in the same direction (240°) for 100 metres to enter a small strip of woodland by electric pole. Pass remnants of old stile. Ignore

Footbridge over M25 at Merstham

stile on right in 100 metres. Continue on indistinct path in woods to stile, over, and soon after through old kissing-gate and then downhill. At bottom, cross lane and go to left of small car-space, by footpath sign, down steps. Ignore stile on left and in a few metres reach lane. Left at lane and pass Quarry Farm on left. Where lane bends left at track junction, go on up track to garage. Over gate to gate ahead, right and to second gate and bridleway sign (349533).

Right on A22 and after 300 metres climb from bridleway sign to bridge. Cross and go on up lane (285°). 150 metres on, at stone bridleway sign, left up bank and continue by side of wood for 400 metres to earth bank, passing groups of firs on right. Here take right path, along bank. After 50 metres, left away from bank along path on the higher of parallel paths. Continue at top of slope, not over the hill, to come out at grassy space and viewpoint (342534).

When grass ends go left past bridleway stone. Take first right fork and at second set of paths take any of three parallel paths ahead (middle one past horse barrier is best). At end, cross stile to cross roads (333532) to go on War Coppice Road, on top of downs, for 1,200 metres. At road junction (Harrow pub is 120 metres on right), cross and go between brick pillars. Along lane to Willey Park Farm, ignoring bridleway on left after 20 metres. When bridleway and lane turn left to farm buildings, keep ahead along track between white posts. Cross road (311542) and along. After 400 metres at metal gate, go half-left down hill (240°) and left of trees. At bottom go through wooden gate and belt of trees. Go down half-right across next field. Right along fence, not through gap, and over gate. Left down to track and into tunnel under M23 (301540).

Left out of tunnel, and after 50 metres, right along field edge. At road right for 200 metres, then left down path between fences. At bottom go half-right across field and cross M25 by footbridge. Right and on path under railway bridge. Left up steps and cross Merstham station by bridge to come out in station yard.

Footpath by Tollsworth Manor, Merstham

Information

Distance	9 miles; total 196 miles. Map 187.
Stations	Hurst Green, Oxted and Woldingham: hourly to Victoria. Merstham: half-hourly, hourly on Sundays, to Victoria.
Buses	London Country 409, 411, and Green Line 719, hourly, Godstone to Caterham on A22.
Refreshments	George, Crown, Old Bell at Oxted, Harrow (327539) at White Hill, Feathers at Merstham.
Accommodation	Difficult. Croydon, Redhill, Reigate.

This final stage gives one of the best walks that can be had anywhere, and provides a fitting finish to the route. There is a lot of climbing, as the way goes alternately on the top and at the bottom of the chalk ridge. But it is worth it for the different views, and the shaded tunnel-like paths through the juniper trees.

The walk starts by going along Quality Street with its old houses, behind the cricket pavilion, and then by a path gradually climbing across the fields. The rich grass makes for comfortable walking, and the bushes at the end are prolific producers of blackberries. The path continues through the grounds of the Royal Alexandra and Albert School, a boarding-school partly run by a foundation and partly by Surrey County Council. Gatton Hall was built by Lord Monson in Italianate style in 1830 and destroyed by fire in 1934, but was rebuilt in the same style by Jeremiah Colman of mustard fame. Lord Monson spent a fortune on embellishing Gatton church with pieces from all over Europe. It is now kept locked and looks sad and neglected, with a curious exterior of pebbledash, brick and stone.

If, where you turned left for the church, you go instead straight ahead through the gates, for 100 metres, you will come to the old Gatton town hall on the right, in a clump of chestnut trees. The hall is an open building about 6 metres by 4 metres, built in 1765 to look like a Grecian temple. Gatton was one of the old 'pocket boroughs', and was entitled to elect two members of parliament, though by the sixteenth century there was sometimes only one elector. The town hall was built so that the election results could be announced there. When the Reform Act of 1832 abolished Gatton's privileges, the then lord of the manor placed the urn in the town hall in grief for the Act's passing.

After Gatton, there is a good path through National Trust woodland which comes out at the car park at the top of Wingate Hill (or Reigate Hill). There is an excellent refreshment stall here, well kept, clean, cheerful and providing good value tea and food—the bread-pudding cake is

especially to be recommended. There are also toilets, and a
bridge over the road to lead to Reigate Hill proper. There is
another temple-like building here, given to Reigate in 1909.
The inside of the roof has blue tiles and a design of the sun,
planets and a twenty-four-hour clock. Unfortunately, none of
the fountains' water-taps or lavatories now works. The grass
on Reigate Hill and the neighbouring Colley Hill is excellent
short turf and it is deservedly popular for picnics. The views
are very good over the town and the little combes descending
to the Weald. At night in balmy summer weather, the lights of
Reigate produce a glittering scene, making the town much
better-looking than in the day. The lights give a glow in the
sky that can be seen for miles.

There is a tricky steep path, with wire ropes to help, from
Colley Hill to the path at the bottom, and then we have a
superb 1½ mile-stretch along the edge of the trees at the
bottom of the Buckland Hills and Juniper Hill. It is like
walking through a tunnel, the junipers and yew grow so
thickly. It is as good in winter, sheltered from the gales, as in
summer, protected from the heat.

After a tricky crossing of the road to Pebble Coombe, we
enter the last stretch from Betchworth to Box Hill. There has
been a good deal of quarrying along here, and the route goes
up and down to avoid the holes left behind. You can see old
limestone kilns and chimneys and can admire the steep chalk
faces. In Brockham Quarry there is now a museum of old
quarry engines and a short stretch of narrow gauge railway on
which they are kept. Work is going on to restore them, and
there are several different types of waggon and engine waiting
their turn for treatment. These engines and quarries were used
for an episode of the TV serial *Doctor Who* to give an
appropriate nightmarish touch! A footpath goes directly
through this museum, but it is not one used by our route,
which looks down on the museum from above.

The chalk slopes have beautiful short turf and, hidden in
the grass, a multitude of small flowers so that the area seems
to stand out with colour in spring and early summer. Leave

Old Gatton Town Hall
Refreshment Stall at Reigate Hill

them there for others also to enjoy. During the ups and downs
the path passes by Quick's grave, where a loved horse was
buried, and above here on the road an hourly bus (not
Sundays) goes to Leatherhead. There is also a pub, the Hand
in Hand. The path past Quick's grave has rather a lot of
rubbish on it from the caravan site above, but we soon leave
this. We have another good stretch on a wide downhill path
through old beeches, before going across the hill and
threading our way through different levels of bush and scrub
to reach Salomon's monument on Box Hill. On the way we
cross a rutted chalk path, the remains of the old Box Hill
road, which in earlier days went from Betchworth to
Leatherhead over Box hill to avoid the Mole valley.

Box Hill is deservedly popular and you are unlikely to have
the grass slopes to yourself. It is a day out for Londoners to
admire the views, sleep on the grass, picnic, play games or just
relax. There is a plan indicator at Salomon's monument
showing the directions of the places you can see—in good
conditions! The best views are after a thunderstorm or on a
dry winter's day. You should be able to pick out Leith Hill
most days, and sometimes, in the distance the South Downs
with the trees of Chanctonbury Ring as the most conspicuous
point.

Box Hill is a big hill and there is lot on it to see. The side
descending to West Humble is a fine grass slope, and is the
one used for skiing. On the top you may find a stone marking
the grave of Major Labelliere, a resident of Dorking who was
buried there upside down. It was his repeated claim that the
world was topsy-turvy and that he should be buried so that
he might be right at last. Juniper Hall over the top is where
Talleyrand stayed after the French Revolution. The novelist
and poet George Meredith lived in Flint Cottage on the
present-day road to the top. The hill has, besides the beeches
we have passed, many yews and, of course, box trees, from
which it derives its name. There are two cafés on the top road,
a Wimpy bar, and, nearer to Salomon's monument, the Fort
tea rooms. These have wooden seats and benches outside and

Footbridge to Reigate Hill
Colley Hill Memorial

provide good tea and cakes to eat on them. Stay for a while
and treat yourself, for you are nearly at the end of the whole
route. There is one quick steep path by the side of the wood,
and then a path wandering through the box trees and
dropping down to the stepping stones over the Mole to the
finish.

You can go along to the Burford Bridge Hotel again to
reclaim your loved ones who have been waiting for you, and
receive their congratulations.

Route

From Merstham station exit by main entrance and bear right
from station to A23 and left to Feathers Inn. Cross road (a
zebra crossing is 100 metres on left) and into Quality Street. 15
metres in, left on footpath to Gatton. Pass cricket pavilion on
left, over stile, then follow fence on left. Continue in same
direction, then go diagonally left uphill to a stile. Then keep
by left fence, later a small wood, past stiles and by an enclosed
path to a road (277532). Right at road and, after 100 metres,
enter and follow drive of Royal Alexandra and Albert school.
Right at chapel, signed to 'Kitchens'. (Left for Gatton church
but straight on to see Gatton town hall.) 50 metres before end
of drive at road, left up track through wood and keep right at
all forks. At road cross to car park and refreshment stall
(263523).

Cross bridge over A217 and follow track for 1,200 metres
past houses on left and mast on right, to Colley Hill and
monument. Keep along top of grassland for 1,200 metres.
Where this ends at National Trust sign by woods, half-left 20
metres before sign, into woods. This soon joins path; go right
along this and steeply downhill. Take second right at track
crossing by horse barrier, and keep to bottom of Juniper Hill,
just above fields for 1½ miles. At T-junction, right up hill for
250 metres, then left down indistinct path, rather hard to find.
There are the remains of a path sign on first tree in on this
path. In 400 metres at T-junction, left downhill and between
fields, under cables, to gate at end strip of woodland—

View of Buckland Hills
Quarry Engine at Brockham Museum

Bridlecombe bungalow on map (218521).

A change has been made here from the original route, for safety reasons on the next road. Go through gate and over stile on right to go on path between lines of trees to reach Pebblehill road. Left on road for 150 metres, cross road carefully, and go on little path on other side of the road, going downhill. Continue till this descends to pavement and in further 300 metres reach post box (210516). (Betchworth station is 300 metres further on.)

Right on track and, after 100 metres, left and past houses. Continue on this track. Cross two tracks and over bridge. Keep to path, ignoring all crossing tracks—path will veer right and then uphill—to top of hill. Near top, opposite corrugated-iron fence on right, left up bank and pass Quick's grave on right (198514). Along winding path just inside wood, and when track comes in from right, go left downhill. After some time reach steps on track. Count them, and at the eleventh step turn right up steep and narrow path. At wide horseshoe-shaped track, take left branch downhill (190510).

The next stage is difficult to describe but many alternatives are possible to get to Box Hill summit. 100 metres after track leaves wood, pass big bush on right. Then 130 metres later, take path right going gently uphill. Continue on this line staying just below scrub line. Path becomes indistinct after 200 metres, but continue on. After 150 metres pass chalky rutted path, and then in 100 metres reach wide path just below scrub. Left 25 metres and then right up bank, across steep hollow and left along path which comes into grassland. Continue up path to trig point (179511) and Salomon's monument. Fort café is on road above on left. Keep on past monument for 300 metres to edge of wood and then steeply downhill by edge of wood to bottom. Right on path into wood and follow orange marks on trees (to Tanners Youth Hostel). At T-junction, go left downhill and after 50 metres, right at hill bottom. Go left of grassy area to Stepping Stones and rejoin the beginning of the Countryway. Cross River Mole by stepping stones—if under water, use bridge 100

Dog and Horse Barrier at foot of Juniper Hill
Yew Path at foot of Buckland Hills

Pilgrims Way Walker
Stepping Stones across River Mole

BOX HILL

metres on right—and keep on to road (171513). Right along
A24 for 500 metres to subway, under road and then uphill
opposite to Box Hill station.

Information

Distance	9 miles; total 205 miles. Map 187.
Stations	Merstham: half-hourly, hourly on Sundays, to Victoria. Betchworth: hourly, two-hourly on Sundays, to Reigate and Dorking. Box Hill: half-hourly, to Victoria.
Buses	London Country 416 Box Hill, from Leatherhead via Headley, hourly, no Sunday service. London Country 470 and Green Line 714, Leatherhead to Dorking on A24, all hourly.
Refreshments	Very good refreshment stall at top Reigate Hill (262523). Hand in Hand at Box Hill village (203520). Wimpy Bar (187512) and Fort tea rooms (178512) at Box Hill.
Accommodation	Tanners Hatch Youth Hostel, Dorking.

Accommodation details are easy to find at two extremes: the
Y.H.A. list youth hostels, and at the expensive end the R.A.C.
and A.A. provide hotel guides. For this reason, I have given
more information on bed-and-breakfast places and cheaper
hotels. However, at this level, changes take place fairly often,
so it is advisable to enquire ahead. There are Tourist Offices at
St Albans, Hertford, Chigwell, Maidstone, Windsor,
Guildford, Maidenhead, Marlow, High Wycombe and
Woking, but these vary considerably in usefulness.

Youth Hostels
There are Youth Hostels at Tanners Hatch (near Box Hill),
Windsor, Bradenham, Lee Gate (near Great Missenden,
Epping Forest and Crockham Hill on the route. Kemsing,
Henley and Harlow could also be useful.

Camping
Besides rough camping, there are camp sites at Horsley,
Chertsey, Rickmansworth, Theobalds Park, Hertford,
Broxbourne, Wrotham, Oldbury Hill and Polesden Lacey.
However, some of these are exclusive to Camping Club
members.

General accommodation
This list is not an exclusive or a recommended list, and
addresses have been obtained from many different sources.

An approximate price category is given, although this is not
guaranteed accurate. As a guide, in 1979, Bed & Breakfast
would be up to £5 in category A, up to £6.50 for B, £8 for C, £10
for D and more than £10 in category E. Single rooms could be
dearer.

*by an address means write or phone before calling.

		Telephone	Price Category
Amersham	Saracens Head, Whielden Street	21958	D
	Ken House Hotel, Long Park	6368	E

	Crown Hotel, Market Square	3344	D
Ascot	Royal Foresters Hotel, London Road	Winkfield Row 4747	E
Berkhamsted	Swan Hotel, High St.	71451	D
	*Mrs Percival, 3 Park View Rd	5436	A
Brentwood	Lion and Lamb Hotel, High St	216427	D
	New World Inn, Gt Warley St	226418	D
	The Brick House, Gt Warley St	217107	C
	Coombe Lodge Country Club, Warley Rd	226687	C
	The Council offices at Brentwood have a short list	228060	
Bulphan	Ye Olde Plough House (Motel)	Grays 891592	E
Chingford	Courtlands Guest House, 28 The Drive, North Chingford	01-529 4834	B
Croydon	Clock House, 47 Brigstock Rd, Thornton Heath	01-684-8480	B
	Swiss Echoes, 7 Birdhurst Rd, S Croydon	01-688 0444	C
	Hayesthorpe House, 52 Augustine's Ave, S Croydon	01-688 8120	C
	Beulah House, 31 Beulah Rd, Thornton Heath	01-653 1788	C
Dorking	Star & Garter, Station Approach	882820	C
	Punch Bowl Motor Hotel	81935/6/7	E
	Acadia Guest House, Cotmandene	882017	A
	*Mrs Dawson, 74 Chalkpit Lane	87952	A
Epping	Treetops, 23/25 Station Rd	73322	D
	Epping Forest Motel, High St	73134	E
Gomshall	The Black Horse Inn	Shere 2242	B
Gravesend	*Mrs Holroyd, 88 Old Rd, East (nr M2)	3904	A
	Clarendon Royal Hotel, Royal Pier Rd	63151	D
Grays	Queens Hotel, High St	72148	C
Guildford	*Mr Parsons, Greyfriars, 9 Castle Hill	61795	A
	Newmans G. H., 24 Waterden Rd	60558	B
	*Mrs Edwards, 104 London Rd	70895	B
	Albany Hotel, 27 London Road	68747	C
	Carlton, 36 London Road	76539	C
	Clavadel, Epsom Rd	72064	E

	Glenariff, 26 Farnham Rd	63875	C
Hatfield	Five Oaks Guest House, Travellers Lane	64168	C
	Hatfield Lodge Hotel, St Albans Rd West	64588	D
	Comet Hotel, 301 St Albans Rd West	65411	E
Hemel Hempstead	Beaconsfield Guest House, 42 Alexandra Rd	42897	B
	Eversleigh Guest House, 40 Alexandra Rd	51366	B
	Southville Guest House, 9 Charles St	51387	B
	Tree Tops Guest House, 37 Alexandra Rd	3530	B
	For address list, write to Tourist Office, the Pavilion, the Marlowes	64451	
Hertford	Tower House, 2 Warren Pk Rd, Bengeo, Hertford	53247	A
	Runton Lodge, 6 Bengeo St, Bengeo, Hertford	53802	B
	Manitoba House, 60 Hertingfordbury Road	53576	B
	Salisbury Arms, Fore St	53091	C
High Wycombe	Belmont Guest House, 9 Priory Ave	27046	A
	Clifton Lodge Hotel, 210 West Wycombe Rd	29062	B
	Drake Court Hotel, 141 London Rd	23639	B
	Oakenbridge Lodge Guest House, 130 West Wycombe Rd	30744	B
Horsley	Mrs Green, Hazelgrove, Epsom Rd West Horsley	East Hursley 4467	A
Kelvedon Hatch	*Mrs Hansell, 15 Glovers Field (*not* week-ends)	Coxtie Green 72381	A
Kings Langley	Eagle Hotel, 127 Hempstead Rd	62563	D
Loughton	St Olave's Hotel, 107 High Rd	01-508 1699	E
Maidenhead	*Mrs Ritchie, Clifton Guest House, Craufurd Rise	23572	C

	Mrs Harvey, Hillrest, 19 Craufurd Rise	20086	B
	Mrs Bolt, Herewards Guest House, Ray Park Avenue	29038	B
	Boulter's Inn, Boulters Lock	21291	E
	Walton Cottage Hotel, Craufurd Rise	24394	E
	Elva Lodge Hotel, Castle Hill	22948	D
Maidstone	*Mrs Jakes, 21 Brewer Street	57858	A
	*Mrs Lungley, 26 Postley Road	58924	A
	Longfield Hotel, 78 London Road	54655	C
	St Michael's Hotel, 4 St Michael's Rd (off Tonbridge Road)	677623	C
	A long list may be obtained from Maidstone Information Centre, The Gatehouse, Old Palace Gdns, Maidstone		
Marlow	Marlow Donkey Hotel, Station Rd	2022	C
	George and Dragon Hotel, The Causeway	3887	D
	Glade Nook Guest House, Glade Rd	4677	D
Oxted	Hoskins, Station Rd, West	2338	E
	Burwood House Hotel, West Hill	3144	C
	*Mrs Higgins, The Rectory, Limpsfield	2512	A
Princes Risborough	Bernard Arms Hotel, Great Kimble	6173	C
	Black Prince Hotel, Wycombe Rd	5076	C
	Rose & Crown, Saunderton	5299	E
	George & Dragon, High St	3087	C
Redhill	Laker's Redstone Hill	61043	D
	Ashleigh House Private Hotel, 39 Redstone Hill	64763	C
Reigate	Norfolk Lodge Guest House, 23 London Rd	48702	C
	Cranleigh, 41 West St	43468	D
	Bridge House Motel, Reigate Hill	46801	E
Rochester	George Inn, 38 High St	Medway 47697	B
	Graystones Guesthouse, 25 Watts Avenue,	Medway 47545	A
	Kings Head Hotel, 58 High St	Medway 42709	E
	Gordon Hotel, 91 High St	Medway 42656	C

	Royal Victoria & Bull Hotel, High St	Medway 46266	D
Romford	Repton Private Hotel, 18 Repton Drive, Gidea Park	Romford 45253	D
Ryarsh	*Mrs Edwards, Heaver House, Chapel St	W Malling 842074	A
St Albans	*Mrs Berry, 1 Samian Gate, King Harry Lane	67378	A
	*Mrs Fuller, 6 Stanhope Rd	56614	A
	*Mrs Hughes, 42 Clarence Rd	53112	A
	*Mrs Osman, 24 Milehouse Close	52570	A
	Crown Hotel, Hatfield Rd	53347	A
	Glenmore House, 16 Woodstock Rd, North	53794	C
	Lower Red Lion, 36 Fishpool St	55669	D
	More addresses are available at the very helpful Tourist Office in 37 Chequer St	64511	
Sevenoaks	The Moorings, Hitchen Hatch Lane	52589	D
	Crown Crest, Seal Rd	54103	D
	Mill House Guest House, Chevening Road, Chipstead	56531	B
	The 74 G.H., Granville Rd	56518	C
	Sevenoaks Park Hotel, Seal Hollow Rd	54245	D
Staines	Pack Horse, Thames St	54221	E
	Swan Hotel, The Hythe	52494	D
Tilbury	Bata Hotel, East Tilbury	2257	B
Ware	Cannons Hotel, Baldock St	5011	E
	Fanhams Hall	5058	E
West Byfleet	Byfleet Hotel	Byfleet 45048	C
West Malling	Swan Hotel, Swan St	843000	C
	*Mrs Clarkson, Birling Lodge, Birling	843724	A
	North View Guesthouse, 2 Church Walk, East Malling	840273	B
West Wycombe	Swan Inn	High Wycombe 27031	B
	George & Dragon (do not book 3–6 p.m.)	High Wycombe 23602	D

Westerham	Kings Arms, Market Square	63246	C
Windsor	*Mrs Warham, 49 Long Mead	66803	A
	*Mrs Todd, 37 Gallys Rd	60708	A
	*Mrs Gates, 29 Upcroft	55960	A
	*Mrs Adams, 59 Clarence Rd	64658	A
	*Mrs Golding, 58 Burnett's Rd	51000	A
	There is a Tourist Office open in the summer at Windsor Central station	52010	
Woking	Croft Ley, 2 Heathside Cresc	72453	C
	North Fleet Hotel, Claremont Av	60350	E
	Wheatsheaf, Horsell	73047	D
	Mayford Manor Hotel	66166	E
Woodford	Torry Glen Hotel, 17 Broomhill Rd, Woodford Green	01-504 5742	C
	Hawthorns Hotel, 83 Wallwood Rd, Leytonstone	01-539 8328	B
Wrotham	Moat Hotel, London Rd, Wrotham	Borough Green 882263	D
	White Rose, London Rd, Wrotham Heath	Borough Green 884149	D

Long Distance Walkers Association

The L.D.W.A. is an organization for those interested in long-distance footpaths, such as the Pennine Way or Offa's Dyke and other walks of at least 20 miles in length. It backed the idea of the London Countryway and its members surveyed the route and helped to produce route descriptions.

The L.D.W.A. organizes and helps with a number of challenge walks where the object is usually to complete a set distance within a time limit, such as the Tanners Marathon, the Downsman Hundred and the Derwent Watershed. It publishes a national magazine about three times a year and a number of local groups have been formed. In the London area, these exist for Kent, Surrey, the Thames Valley, Essex and Herts. Membership is open to all for £1.75 a year. Details from the Membership Secretary, 4 Mayfield Rd, Tunbridge Wells, Kent, TN4 8ES.

Ramblers Association

The Ramblers Association is the organization for all those interested in preserving footpaths, public access to the countryside and fighting for the rights of the walker. It is long established and has been growing rapidly in recent years, with over 32,000 members now. It has over a hundred local groups, including several in the London area, which organize social rambles and work to preserve footpaths. Membership is £3.50 a year. Details from the Ramblers Association, 1/5 Wandsworth Road, London, SW8 2LJ

Youth Hostels Association

The Y.H.A. has over two hundred and fifty hostels in England and Wales, with ten near the Countryway route. All hostels provide simple dormitory accommodation, but vary greatly in other ways. The cost of an overnight stay depends on the person's age and the type of hostel, but, with a few exception, is between £1.50 and £2.40 for bed and breakfast. Membership is open to all with *no* upper age limit, for £2.65 a year, age sixteen to twenty for £1.60, and under sixteen for

90p. National office is Trevelyan House, 8 St Stephen's Hill, St Albans, Herts., AL1 2DY.

Camping Club
The Camping Club looks after the interests of campers and has a number of sites, some owned by it, for its members' exclusive use. Several of these are near the London Countryway route. Membership is £9.00 a year, with an entrance fee of £1.50. Details from its headquarters at 11 Grosvenor Place, London SW1. Telephone: 01-828 1012.

All references are to page numbers; those in italics are to maps, those in **bold** are to illustrations.